THE DARLING PEPPERBOX

The Story of Sam Colt's Forgotten Competitors in Bellingham, Massachusetts and Woonsocket, Rhode Island

by Stuart C. Mowbray

editor of *Man at Arms* magazine

photography and artwork by the author unless otherwise indicated

---

MOWBRAY PUBLISHING, P.O. BOX 460, LINCOLN, RI 02865 USA

LIBRARY OF CONGRESS
CONTROL NUMBER: 2003114316
    Stuart C. Mowbray
    The Darling Pepperbox: The Story of Sam Colt's Forgotten Competitors in
    Bellingham, Massachusetts and Woonsocket, Rhode Island
    Lincoln, R.I.: ANDREW MOWBRAY INCORPORATED — PUBLISHERS
    104 pp.

ISBN: 1-931464-11-1

© 2004 Stuart C. Mowbray

All rights reserved. No part of this book may be reproduced in any form
or by any means without permission in writing from the publisher.

To order more copies of this book, or to receive a free catalog
of other fine arms collecting publications, call 1-800-999-4697 or 401-726-8011.
Email us at orders@manatarmsbooks.com or visit our web page at www.manatarmsbooks.com

Printed in Canada.
This book was designed and set in type by Stuart C. Mowbray.

First Edition

9 8 7 6 5 4 3 2 1

About the covers: Front cover photography courtesy of Little John's Auctions and the Kim M.
Mowbray collection of Woonsocket memorabilia. Back cover photography by Stuart C.
Mowbray; pistols from the collection of Howard Miller.

The Contents

Dedication   5
Acknowledgments   6
Introduction   7

The Places 9

The People 17

A Visit to the
Darling Pistol Factory 49

The Pistols 57

The Darling–Colt Connection 89

The Tools in the
Darling Probate List 93

Bibliography   98
Endnotes   101

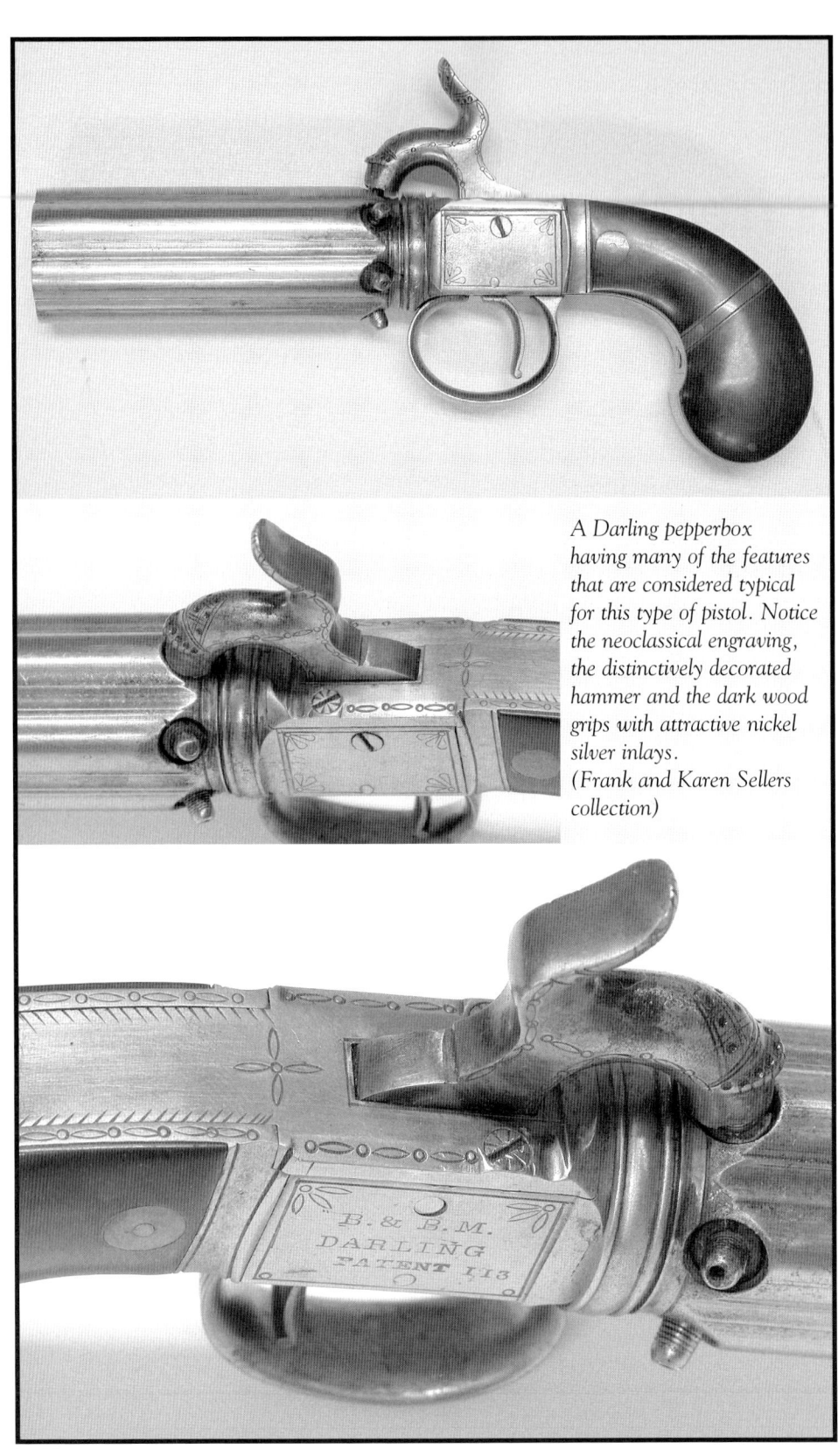

A Darling pepperbox having many of the features that are considered typical for this type of pistol. Notice the neoclassical engraving, the distinctively decorated hammer and the dark wood grips with attractive nickel silver inlays.
(Frank and Karen Sellers collection)

Dedication

This book is dedicated to Howard Miller, who has what I believe to be the best Darling pepperbox collection ever assembled. He is also a true gentleman and I doubt that I would ever have bothered to publish my research on this topic without his encouragement.

Acknowledgments

Even a little book like this one requires the assistance and advice of many people. I wish to thank Richard Littlefield, Joe Puleo, Nick Chandler, Pete Schmidt, Frank Sellers, Robert Howard, Ernie Taft, Charles L. Foster, Norm Flayderman, Herbert G. Houze, R.L. Wilson, Bob Berryman, John Gangel, Greg Martin, the residents of Wrentham Road in Bellingham, Mass., the members of the Massachusetts Arms Collectors and the American Society of Arms Collectors.

 I also wish to acknowledge the staffs of the Harris Public Library in Woonsocket, R.I., the Rhode Island Historical Society Library, the Providence Public Library, the Pawtucket Public Library, the Cumberland Public Library, the Bellingham Public Library, the University of Rhode Island Library, the Cody Firearms Museum and Library, the Woonsocket Museum of Work and Culture, the City and Town Clerks for Woonsocket, Bellingham, Smithfield, Cumberland, Central Falls, Shrewsbury and Norfolk County, the Mormon Family History Library, and the Providence branch of the U.S. Patent Office.

 Finally, I would like to thank my wife Kim and my daughter Miranda, who have put up with an inexcusable number of "family trips" to archives, libraries, swamps and graveyards so that this book could be as complete and accurate as possible.

Introduction

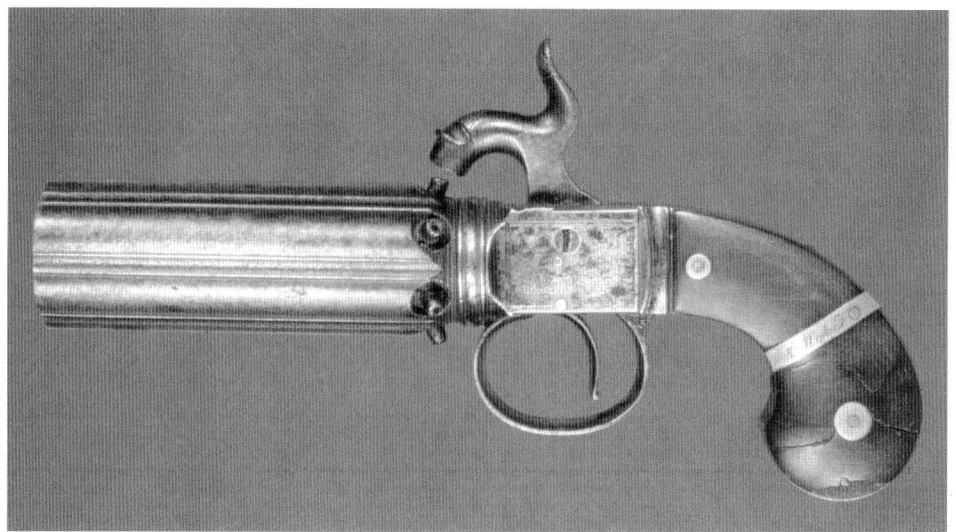

A Darling pepperbox in very good, unrestored condition. This is the pistol that was invented by Barton and Benjamin M. Darling. First made in Bellingham, Massachusetts, it is thought that the pistols were also made at a later time in Woonsocket, Rhode Island. This pistol is considered a pepperbox because it has six barrels that rotate as a group. Each barrel has its own percussion cap and was fired individually, as can be seen in the photograph. (Howard Miller collection)

The history of small-time gunmaking is full of spectacular failures, but the Darling brothers took it one step further. They failed with attitude. They came so close to fame and fortune that it almost seemed like an ironic insult. Both of the gunmakers to whom the Darlings are commonly compared (Samuel Colt and Ethan Allen) became icons and men of wealth, while the Darlings both died unknown and insolvent.

The pistol invented and manufactured by Barton and Benjamin M. Darling was of the "pepperbox" type. Pepperboxes are defined as a pistol with four or more barrels bunched in a circle so that they rotate as a group around a central axis. While there are a few very old flintlock guns fitting this general description, these never gained widespread popularity. The type usually called pepperboxes today were percussion pistols first experimented with in the 1830s. When the Darlings received the very first American patent for a pepperbox in 1836, it was considered an innovative item. As far as pepperboxes go, Darlings were part of the experimental phase for that style of gun, which was still a few years and a few improvements away from becoming the newest and "hottest" type of gun to carry for personal protection. However, it was not the Darlings who would discover these improvements nor would they benefit from the vast popularity of pepperbox pistols during the 1840s and beyond.

Today, the pepperbox pistols made by the Darling brothers are amongst the rarest American-made firearms, and a generation ago they were perhaps the most sought after. Some authors have claimed that they are *the* rarest production firearm ever made in America, although I am quite sure that this is not true. Aside from being rare, Darlings are intriguing because they revolve their cylinder (barrel cluster) upon cocking. This feature is the single most important part of Sam Colt's revolver invention and it has been suggested by many that the Darlings were the first to make this revolutionary innovation, despite the fact that Colt filed his patent papers a little earlier.

The popularity of Darlings amongst collectors began with the late Sam Smith. Perhaps the most influential pistol collector of the post-World War II era, Smith loved Darlings and shared this enthusiasm with his many friends and protégés. Prices for the few discovered examples of this "holy grail" reached record amounts, in some cases being so high that they have only been surpassed in the last few years. Nowhere was this frenzy more alive than in the prestigious American Society of Arms Collectors, where Smith and his fellow members made Darlings the true darling of the gun collecting world.

Smith, himself, did a great deal of research on Darling pepperboxes, which were poorly understood. Little was known about these pistols beyond the patent drawing, and it is to Smith that we must credit most of the previously published information on these weapons, whether correct or not. He went to great lengths to discover information about the Darling brothers. He even hired local researchers, yet discovered frustratingly little, not even where they lived and worked. I believe that I have added significantly to the story, but this was only possible because I live where the Darlings did and have all the resources at hand. Smith put in an impressive amount of work on this subject and it is a pleasure and an honor to follow in his footsteps. *Stuart C. Mowbray*

The Places

All of the events in this story take place in Bellingham, Massachusetts and Woonsocket, Rhode Island — two communities that meet at the very top of Rhode Island where it touches Massachusetts. Strangely, the actual location of the border line between these two states remained in dispute into relatively modern times, with no one bothering to resolve the question until the governors of each state eventually met at a tavern and settled the matter over a drink. The Darlings lived in this disputed zone of land and probably considered themselves citizens of both states. Technically, they first lived in Bellingham, Massachusetts, and later moved to Woonsocket, Rhode Island, but both locations were within walking distance of each other and were intertwined communities.

A description of the area under discussion is difficult. The land fell (and to some great extent still falls) into two basic categories: farmland and mill villages. For the purposes of this story, it is easiest to think of Bellingham as the farmland and Woonsocket as the mill village, but the reality was actually more complicated than that, with pastures being just a stone's throw from densely industrialized riversides. This interesting interweaving of fields and factories meant that you could have rural farmland with a pure "cows and crops" mentality, but within short walking distance of burgeoning industrial centers where advanced mechanical skills and state-of-the-art machinery were commonplace.

The best early account of Bellingham is found in the small book *Confessions of Boyhood,* by John Albee. He tells us that, "The traveller, journeying through the highways of Bellingham, would see nothing to attract his attention or interest. It has no monuments, ruins nor historic associations; no mountain, nor hill even... The soil is stony and pays back not much more than is put into it. The fine forests of white oak have been mostly reduced to ashes... No eminent sons have yet remembered the town with noble benefactions. It has had no poet and no mention in literature. The reporters pass it by. It is not even a suburb, last sad fate of many towns and villages... Before cities and factories had begun to stir the ambition and attract the young by opportunities for fortune and fame, Bellingham was the home of an intelligent, liberty-loving people. It was the best place in the world to be born in."

Bellingham did eventually have its share of industry, but most of that happened far north of Wrentham Road where the Darlings lived and worked. However, south-central Massachusetts was amok with gunmakers in the 1800s, so despite their rural location, the Darlings would have had plenty of interaction with other members of their trade. In fact, the most famous pepperbox maker of all time, Ethan Allen, was also a native of Bellingham, leading to justifiable speculation that Allen worked for one or another of the Darlings at some point in his early career, perhaps developing an enthusiasm for pepperboxes in the process. However, most of the Darlings' neighbors were farmers and the biggest landmark in the area was a tavern down the road where coaches used to stop on their way between larger towns. Even today, there is a lot of pasture land along Wrentham Road with small farms alongside of an increasing number of newly constructed houses. As will be shown later, this portion of Southern Bellingham was so far from the center of town and so close to Woonsocket that when residents went "into town" it must have been to Woonsocket that they were heading. Eventually, many Bellingham residents, including the Darlings, simply moved there.

New England was industrializing rapidly during these years and water power meant everything. The major source of power in this region was the Blackstone River. This dynamic, twisting river was the birthplace of the textile industry in the United States, much like the Connecticut River was the birthplace of the firearms industry. The once-tiny village of Woonsocket (also called Woonsocket Falls) within the town borders of Cumberland, R.I., had the largest drop on the entire Blackstone River and quickly became a "cotton fever" boom town attracting several major manufacturers of cotton and woolen goods. When the Darlings lived there, Woonsocket Falls was theoretically still part of purely agricultural Cumberland, yet the mills and housing had spread across the river to land that was part of another agricultural community called Smithfield. This was an arrangement that became increasingly uncomfortable as the "village" rapidly developed into the single most industrialized city in America, straddling the river and vastly overshadowing the farm towns in which it was located. It would eventually break away and be incorporated as the City of Woonsocket in the 1880s.

An almanac for the year 1844 describes Woonsocket Falls as a "thriving manufacturing village... The streets are irregularly laid out and there is but little uniformity in the architecture of the buildings. The

The roar of Woonsocket Falls — the largest source of power on the Blackstone River. This early photograph shows how beautiful the scenery could be right in the midst of the booming textile industry.
(Kim Mowbray collection)

scenery in the vicinity, however, is grand and picturesque." The population was listed at 4,000 and the village was reported to have five churches, one bank, one newspaper, three attorneys, two dentists, three physicians, three public houses, twelve grocery stores, eight dry goods stores, three hardware stores and fifteen textile mills. The mills employed a total of 885 hands and were growing exponentially.[1]

What exactly was Woonsocket like when the Darlings were making their pistols? Much like boom towns in the West, it must have been a bit on the rough-and-ready side, in stark contrast to the picturesque scenery of the outlying landscape described above.

One visitor to Woonsocket, Thomas Man, stayed there for two to three months in 1835 and was so offended that he wrote and published a whole book describing his experiences. He even sent a copy to the Library of Congress, where it is still preserved today.

Man describes himself as a "Professor of Eloquence and The Languages" and quickly shows himself to be a self-important snob. I am willing to bet that he was unbearable at dinner parties. However, he was a keen observer and what he describes is a raw industrial settlement thrown up around mills much like Western goldrush towns were thrown up around mines. And like miners, these early industrialists were learning (and making up) the rules as they went along. He begins:[2]

Woonsocket is in size an overgrown factory village containing about 2,500 inhabitants — situated on the romantic Blackstone River; — its location on this earth has been accidental; without order or design, and unpremeditated, extremely rough, sandy, barren and unproductive as the great desert of Sahara.

The author of nature has, however, fitted the inhabitants to the soil in its chaotic state; being devoid of all the common social feelings of humanity and everything which renders life amiable. Like the merciless Arabs, preying on one another, and when a favorable opportunity presents itself, committing depredations on the unsuspecting traveler; sunk in the lowest state of barbarity and mental degradation...

...The only hotel, if we may be allowed to debase the term by calling it so, is kept by a very mercenary, avaricious and senseless man, whose sole object is making money, without any regard to the comfort and pleasure of the traveler. The house is built in very bad taste, and in every way incommodious, he being the architect... There is, however, one fine thing in the kitchen — a large sink opening in the floor, dark as the hole of Calcutta, where all the filth of the house is emptied and carried off below by SILVER PIPES.

The table is served in the most barbarous style, as you will scarcely ever find a decent piece of meat on it which could be masticated with common good teeth — the beef steak being always cut from the thigh or neck of a bullock, consequently cheaper. And never half cooked, the fresh blood still dripping from it... The yard before the door is ever animated by the presence of a great variety of swine, of every color, like Laban's sheep — ring streaked and speckled — attracted there no doubt by something like fellow-feeling.

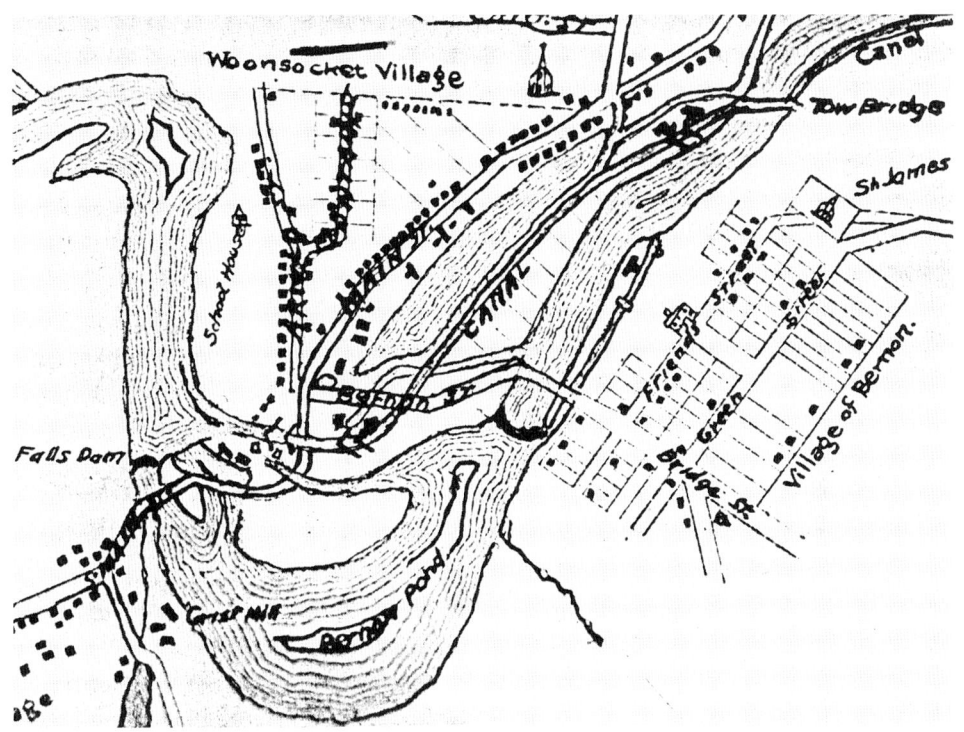

An 1838 map of the village of Woonsocket Falls, Rhode Island. Notice how the Blackstone River dominates the scene. Portions of the map above the river show land owned by the town of Cumberland; portions of the map below the river show land owned by the town of Smithfield. The village began in Cumberland, but as industry grew there was increasing development on the Smithfield side of the river. Bellingham, Massachusetts, is just off the map to the north. (Cumberland Public Library History Collection)

I live in Woonsocket and while I am sure that things have changed over the past hundred and seventy years, the quality of some of the local restaurants certainly has not. Historian A.P. Thomas has suggested that the silver pipes mentioned above were actually a mill trench opening and that the waste was being dumped into the spillway that carried the water already used by water wheels and directed its flow back into the main river. But Mr. Man continues:

In this place is also a Church [Baptist Meeting House], resembling rather the school-house of a factory village, built on an elevated site; raised like a beacon on high, to warn sinners from afar, to flee from the wrath to come and to shed its spiritual light around, where the unfledged theological student sometimes enters, to whet his beak, and stretch his spiritual wings.

Another rare, early photographic view of Woonsocket Falls. This is the scene that author Thomas Man described as "majestic grandeur...filling the soul with the most sublime and awful emotions."
(Kim Mowbray collection)

[There is also] a weekly newspaper from which emanates, ever and anon, gleams of light to illuminate the path of the natives, groping in moral, intellectual and religious darkness...

Man goes on to complain about children working in the factories, the number of Jews in town, incompetent doctors, slovenly ministers and the like. He also saves some special venom for a mill superintendent Weevelly who is described as "brutal, savage, ferocious, without mercy, vile, dirty, squalid, insignificant, contemptible, dastardly, barbarous, malignant and wretched." He obviously made an impression. Man sums up:

Almost the only thing that can attract and entertain the eye of the traveler is the lofty cataract [waterfall], tumbling in majestic grandeur over the rugged rocks, roaring and foaming in the immense and unfathomable abyss below, from whose sprays are formed under a clear and serene sky ten thousand rainbows, filling the soul with the most sublime and awful emotions.

In the Indian language, Woonsocket means "thundermist." Today the falls are controlled by dams and flood prevention devices, but originally they were spectacular as can be seen from the photo above.

This is the unique environment in which the Darling pepperbox was invented and built — a mixture of farmland, rural splendor, dangerous factories, crude accommodations, rough manners and history-making technical innovation. This description could be repeated for countless other developing towns all across the American Northeast, that were riding the wave of the industrial revolution for all it was worth.

Before moving on to other topics, it should be mentioned that some books and articles have said that the Darlings also made pepperboxes in Shrewsbury, Massachusetts. Where this information came from is left unexplained, but it was probably a pet theory of arms historian Sam Smith. Frank Sellers, while researching his exceptional study *American Gunsmiths*, found no evidence to support a Shrewsbury connection. I searched the same sources independently and also found nothing. My current belief is that the pepperboxes were never made in Shrewsbury and that the Darlings never worked there. An inspection of the documents cited later will show that the Darlings used their Bellingham address consistently in all discovered paperwork and advertisements from before the pistol invention until 1839 when their address immediately switched to Woonsocket and stayed there. There are no gaps in the historical record into which a Shrewsbury venture would seem to fit. Also, all of the Darlings' businesses and residences fall into an area of about four square miles at the most. These were local boys who stayed within walking distance of their birthplace. A distant manufacturing location makes little sense when so much water power and skilled labor were available in their own neighborhood.

The Darling Pepperbox

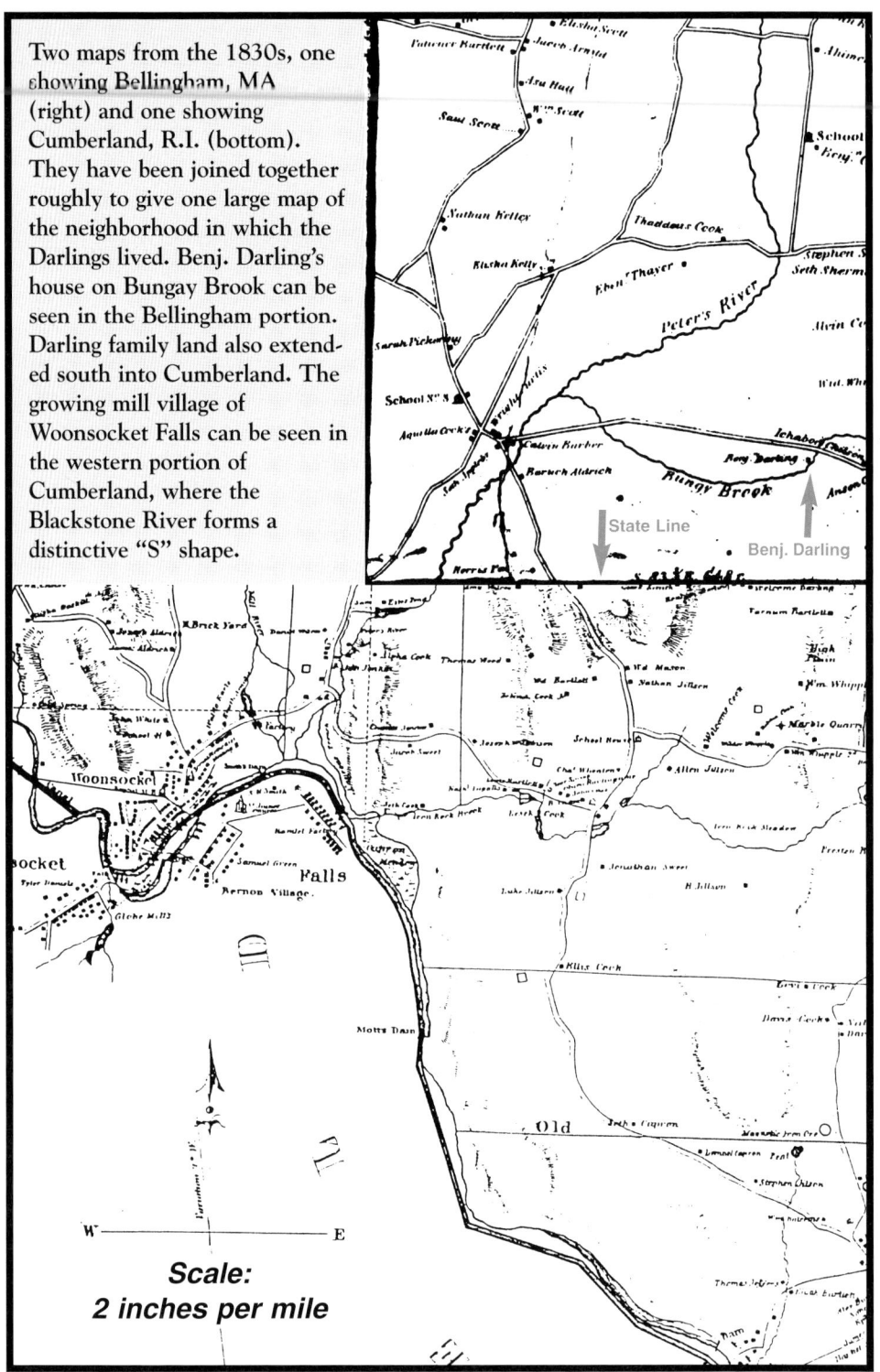

Two maps from the 1830s, one showing Bellingham, MA (right) and one showing Cumberland, R.I. (bottom). They have been joined together roughly to give one large map of the neighborhood in which the Darlings lived. Benj. Darling's house on Bungay Brook can be seen in the Bellingham portion. Darling family land also extended south into Cumberland. The growing mill village of Woonsocket Falls can be seen in the western portion of Cumberland, where the Blackstone River forms a distinctive "S" shape.

Scale: 2 inches per mile

The People

Since Woonsocket, Rhode Island, was an as-of-yet unincorporated city developing in a remote corner of the rural town of Cumberland, overflowing into neighboring Smithfield, and sharing a disputed border with Bellingham, Massachusetts, it is quite natural that historical records concerning early citizens are confusing and hard to locate. People in this disputed zone between the two states did their business at their own convenience, filing land deeds in one town, receiving their mail in a second, and perhaps going through probate in a third. In essence, they acted as citizens of both states with no respect for the convenience or sanity of modern-day researchers.

This problem is further complicated in the case of the Darlings, who were a large and important "old line" family. There were 115 members of the Darling family born in Bellingham before 1850 alone, with even more family members in Cumberland and other surrounding towns. They often used identical first names, Benjamin being particularly popular, and many were mechanics or mill operators.

However, despite these challenges, a basic outline of their lives has emerged. The inventors of the Darling pepperbox, Barton and Benjamin M. Darling, were the children of Benjamin and Lavina (Jillson) Darling. Both parents came from families with long histories in Cumberland, and they were married in that town on November 18, 1798.[3] The new husband was listed as the son of Peter Darling, and described as a mechanic.[4] The couple had seven children, Barton being the first (born July 31, 1799) and Benjamin M. being the fifth (born September 29, 1809).[5] Benjamin M. Darling would, throughout his life, use the middle initial "M." to distinguish himself from his father, who simply went as "Benjamin." In this book, we will follow this example and include Benjamin M.'s middle initial whenever we refer to him. Any reference to a Benjamin without the middle initial refers to his father. It sounds a little awkward, but it avoids confusion.

A search of the U.S. Census results for Cumberland confirms the growth of the Darling family. In 1800, the Benjamin Darling household lists two "Free White Males" (one under age 10 and one age 26-45) and

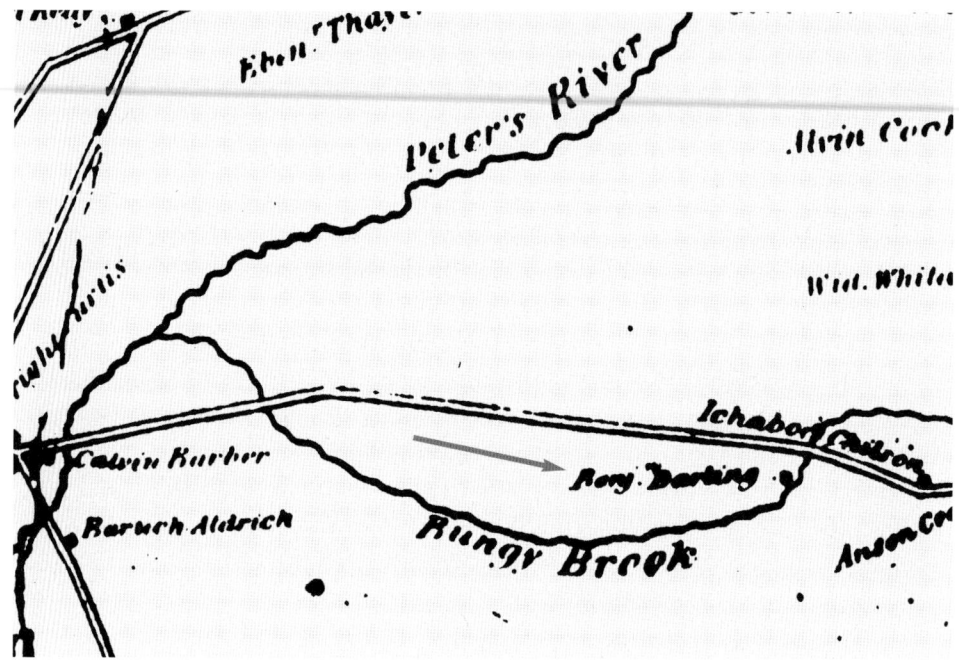

An enlargement of the map shown previously, showing "Benj. Darling's" homestead and gunsmith shop (see arrow) on Bungay Brook. The road was called the Highway to Wrentham and is now called Wrentham Road. Notice that Ichabod Chilson's house is shown across the street and to the east. Later we will learn that Chilson is the farmer who sold Barton Darling the rights to build a dam on his land. Water from this dam would power the Darling pepperbox factory. (Bellingham Historical Commission)

one "Free White Female" (age 16-26). The 1820 Census shows five "Free White Males" (one age 10-16, one age 16-18, two age 18-26 and one age 45+) and two "Free White Females" (one age 10-16 and one age 26-45). In 1820, one member of the household is listed as "engaged in agriculture" and three as "engaged in manufacturing."[6]

Benjamin appears to have been moderately prosperous from the very beginning, as he was able to purchase land as early as 1801.[7] On March 18, 1805, Benjamin bought "a small piece or tract of land with the remains of an old Blacksmith Shop thereon standing, containing by estimation one acre and three quarters...with the...privilege to pass and repass from said shop to the Highway through Esuk Cook's land..."[8] This location was on Bungay Brook (sometimes spelled Bungy or Bungey), a branch of Peter's River, and alongside property that was already owned by other members of

Darling's family. Since blacksmith shops did not generally require water power, it is assumed that this shop was not powered by the brook, which today does not generate nearly enough force to drive a water wheel. The exact trade Darling undertook at his shop is not listed in any records, although it was almost certainly gunsmithing as his estate at the time of his death included many gunsmithing tools including "1 wrought iron anvil; 1 cast iron anvil; 2 rifling rods; one iron vice; one iron bar; 10 gun barrel reamers; 1 gun; 2 powder horns...", etc.[9]

In March of 1820, Benjamin was gifted by his brother a very large parcel of land that was either connected to or within sight of the parcel where his shop was located. Not only had this land been in the Darling family for generations, but all of the Darlings who owned it had been metalworkers and apparently practiced their trades there.[10] The land had entered the Darling family in 1727, when Richard Darling, a blacksmith, purchased 25 acres on Bungay Brook. When Benjamin received it from his brother many generations later, it was described in the deed as "a certain tract of land, situated lying and being in Cumberland...and the largest part being in Bellingham...one dwelling house and corn house standing."[11] Benjamin moved his family into this dwelling house, which remains standing today on Wrentham Road in Bellingham. An 1830 map shows Benjamin Darling's homestead, set back from the road alongside Bungay Brook. This was a considerable piece of farmland that had been tilled by the Darlings for generations. It was at this location that Benjamin's pepperbox-inventing sons enter the historical record.

Benjamin Darling had three sons who lived to adulthood: Barton, Alvin and Benjamin M. All three of them followed in their father's footsteps as mechanics, and they were all inventors as well. Barton, as the eldest, was the first to establish himself in the world by operating a shop on his father's land along Wrentham Road. Barton, as well as being a machinist or mechanic, is also listed as a "machine maker" on some legal documents, which implies a higher level of expertise. By all indications, he was the genius of the family. On June 6, 1833, he purchased a small piece of land from his neighbor Ichabod Chilson, who lived across the street and up the road to the east of the Darling homestead. Chilson was a farmer and "sything-man," meaning that he worked for the town on a three-man team cutting the grass and bramble from roadsides.[12] The deed is worth quoting because it describes what would later become the Darling pistol factory:

I Ichabod Chilson, yeoman, ...do hereby convey unto...Barton Darling a small tract of land laying in said Bellingham, containing about ten rods of land for the purpose of building a dam across Bungey Brook, so called, for the purpose of making a resovor [sic] to hold water for the benefit of his mill or shop below. ...the said Barton Darling agrees to build a good and lasting dam across said brook, which is to be six feet high or more. Said dam is to be built of stone and gravel and the stones are to be taken in the lot near by and the gravel to be taken on the north side of the [nearby] ditch, and the said Chilson reserving the right to use all the waste water that the said Darling does not use for the use of his shop for the purpose of watering his land and to draw the water south end of said dam.[13]

An 1858 map shows what was done. Barton was arranging to power a mill alongside his father's. Whether his father continued at the old location or joined his son to take advantage of this new power is unclear. What is clear is that a reservoir and dam (shown with an arrow on the right of the map below) were constructed on the north side of the road and a trench built off of the west side of the dam, cutting across the road

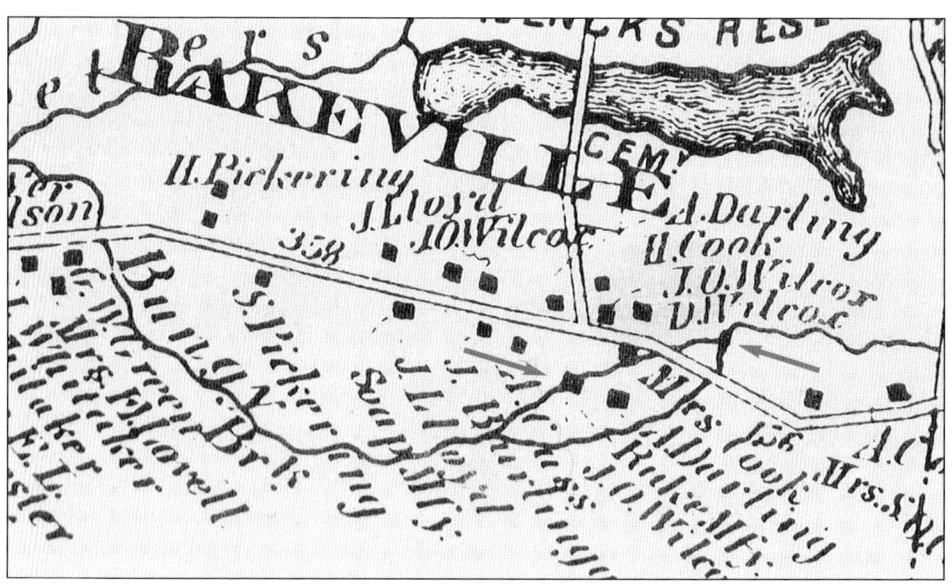

An 1876 map of Bellingham, showing the Darlings' neighborhood enlarged. If you compare this map to the map shown two pages earlier, you can see that Barton's trench has been added above Bungay Brook. As will be discussed later, the rectangle in the center of the trench, between the road and where the trench re-enters the brook, is where the pistol factory was located. Arrows are added to show the dam and factory. (Bellingham Historical Commission)

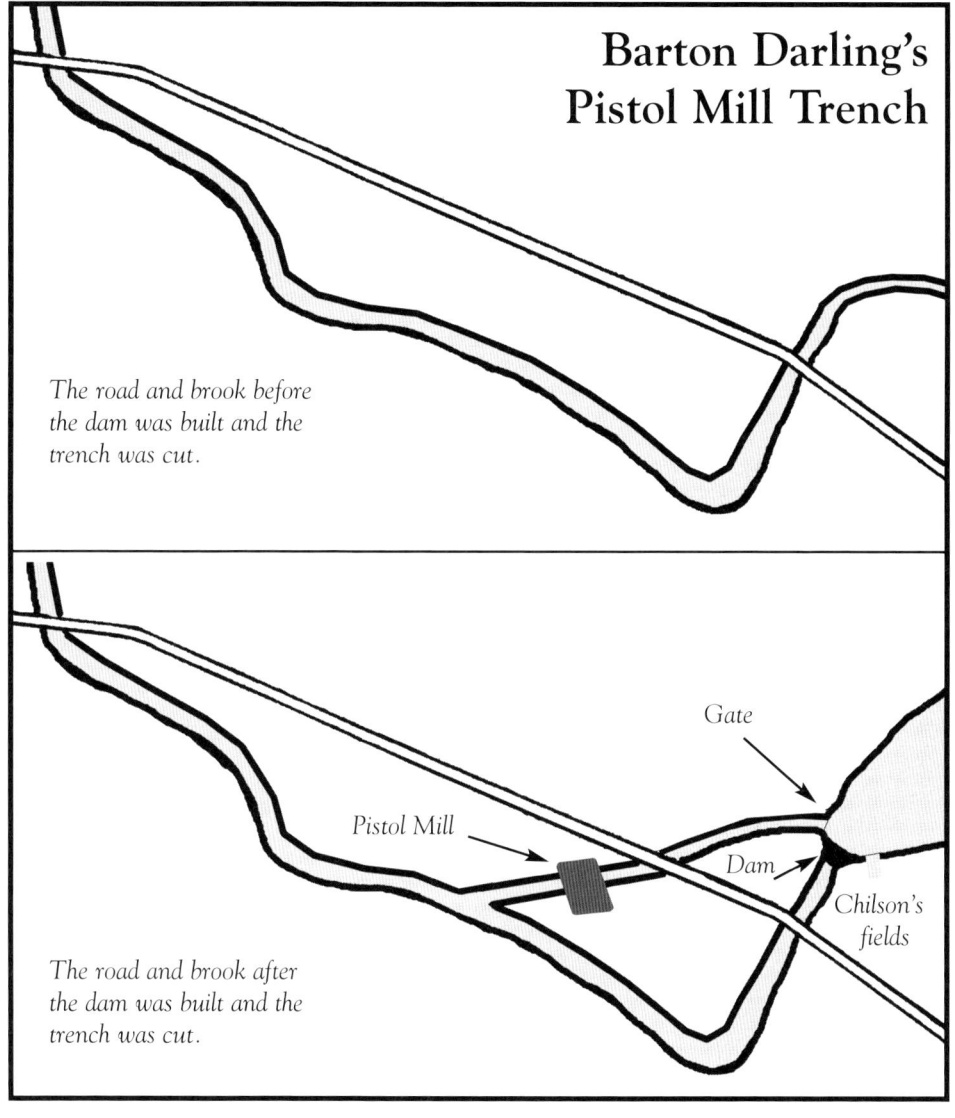

As a result of land deals with Ichabod Chilson and others, Barton Darling was able to build a six-foot stone dam on Bungay Brook, to the north of the Highway to Wrentham. He then built a trench which brought water to his pistol mill. The water would eventually spill back into the brook. Chilson retained the right to drain unneeded water from the reservoir to irrigate his fields. There would have been a gate where the trench exited the reservoir. This gate would have allowed Darling to shut off the water for repairs and during idle periods. This gate also would have had a crude filter on it called a "trash rack" to keep out floating wood and other debris. (Inept artwork by the author)

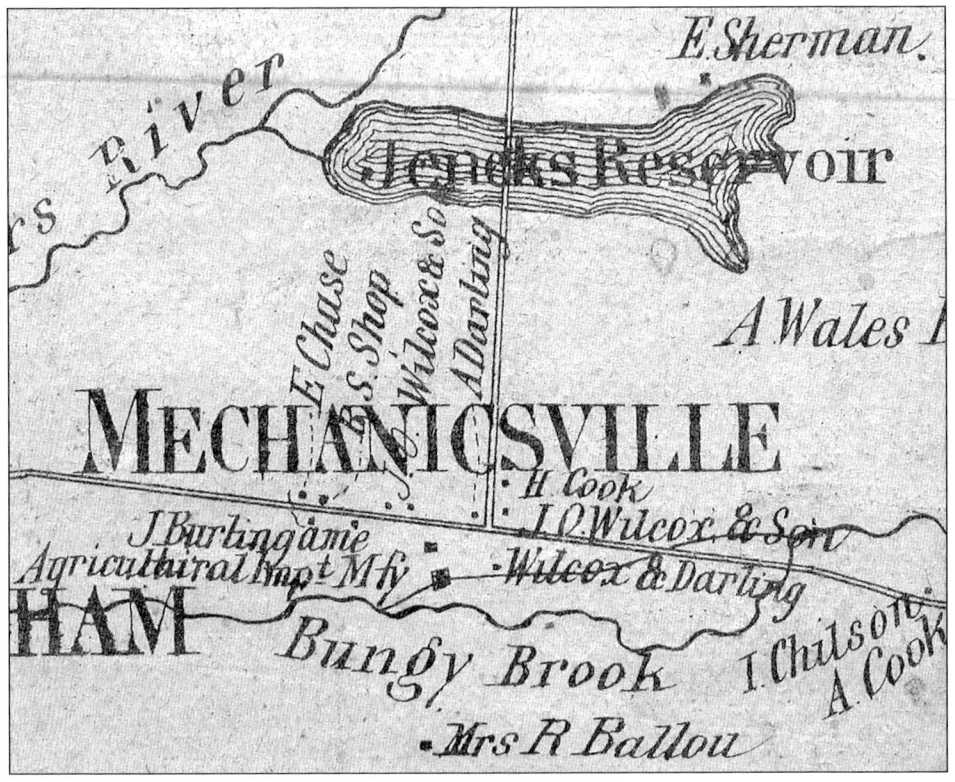

to the northwest of the brook and eventually rejoining and spilling back into the brook itself. Barton's mill would have been built on the land that he owned along this trench on the south side of the road. This was a common way of directing water power with the trench bringing a compressed stream of plunging water to exactly where Barton needed it. Note that the map refers to this area as Mechanicsville, doubtless in direct reference to the Darlings themselves. Chilson reserved the right to draw extra water for his fields from the south end of the dam; this was across the dam from Barton's trench gate and convenient to Chilson's fields and house on that side of the brook.

Barton made many other real estate transactions during this period, all of which appear to have been in the immediate neigh-

(above) An even earlier map, 1858, showing Barton's trench. The trench can be seen above the brook and crossing the Highway to Wrentham. Ichabod Chilson's house can be seen just above the road at the extreme right. (Bellingham Historical Commission, with thanks to Ernie Taft)

(right) The original deed between Chilson and Barton Darling, detailing the transaction that allowed dam and trench construction.

Know all Men by these Presents,

THAT I Ichabod Chilson of Bellingham in the County of Norfolk and Commonwealth of Massachusetts Yeoman,

in consideration of five dollars

paid by Barton Darling of Bellingham in the County and Commonwealth aforesaid Machinist

the Receipt whereof I do hereby acknowledge, do hereby give, grant, sell and convey unto the said Barton Darling a small tract of land laying in said Bellingham, containing about ten rods of land for the purpose of building a dam across Bungey Brook, so called, for the purpose of making a resovoy to hold water for the benefit of my mill or shop below, bounded as follows, beginning at the ditch where the water now runs by Molley Clarks land, then southerly on said Clarks land to the brook above named, then crossing said brook, southerly and running six rods on said Clarks land, then westerly twelve feet, then northerly to the ditch above mentioned, then easterly on said bank twelve feet to the bound first above mentioned, and in lieu of paying the consideration of five dollars as above, the said Barton Darling agrees to build a good and lasting dam across said brook, which is to be six feet high or more — said dam is to be built of stone and gravel and the stones are to be taken in the lot near by and the gravel to be taken on the north side of the above said ditch, and the said Chilson reserving the right to use all the waste water that. The said Darling does not use for the use of his shop for the purpose of watering his land and to draw the water south end of said dam. —

TO HAVE AND TO HOLD the afore-granted premises to the said Barton Darling his heirs and assigns to their use and behoof forever.

AND I do covenant with the said Barton Darling his heirs and assigns, that I am lawfully seized in Fee of the afore-granted Premises: That they are free of all Incumbrances: That I have good right to sell and convey the same to the said Barton Darling his heirs and assigns & to their use.

And that I will warrant and defend the same premises to the said Barton Darling his heirs and assigns forever, against the lawful claims and demands of all persons.

In Witness Whereof, I the said Ichabod Chilson

have hereunto set my Hand and Seal this sixth day of June in the year of our Lord One thousand eight hundred and thirty three

Signed, sealed and delivered in presence of us,

John Bates
Samuel L. Hobbs

Ichabod Chilson (Seal)

Norfolk ss. June the 6th 1833 Then Ichabod Chilson personally acknowledged the above instrument to be his free act and deed—before me,

John Bates, Justice of the Peace.

Dedham December 23. 1835
Rec'd Enters & Exam'd
by Enos Foora Reg

The Darling Pepperbox

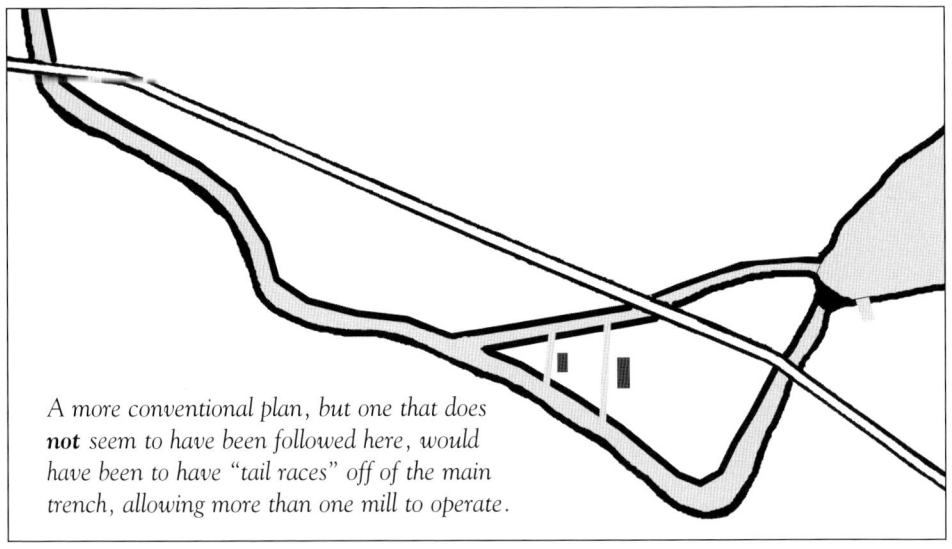

A more conventional plan, but one that does **not** seem to have been followed here, would have been to have "tail races" off of the main trench, allowing more than one mill to operate.

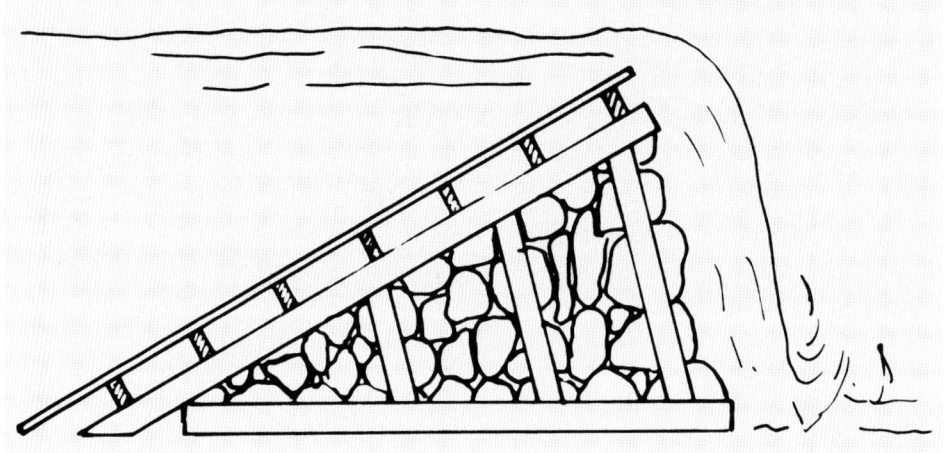

A modern drawing showing how waterfalls were constructed in the 19th century. A timber frame was filled with rocks. The front face of the waterfall was often finished like a fine stone wall. The brooks and streams of New England are littered with waterfalls of this type, although the mills themselves are often gone. (Courtesy Robert Howard)

borhood of his father's house and adjoining his father's land.[14] While the wording of these deeds is often unclear, all of these purchases were probably related to his mill and many of them were doubtless small purchases of land needed to allow passage of his trench. One of the deeds mentions that the land being purchased included a ditch "for the purpose of carrying the water in said ditch into the natural stream [Bungay Brook]." This ditch carried the runoff from his mill's trench after the water had been used by the water wheel. Such a ditch is often called a "spillway" or a "tail race." Now in his 30s, Barton published his intention to marry Persis Smith on September 27, 1835.[15] Persis would remain his wife until he died, and her name appears on many of his legal documents as a co-signer.

It may surprise some gun collectors that the Darling pepperbox was not the first invention patented and manufactured by Barton Darling. His first patent was with his other brother, Alvin (who was five years his junior and sometimes spelled his name Alvan).[16] It was dated April 3, 1835, and covers a cast and wrought-iron water wheel that they called a Spiral Pressure Wheel. This particular style of wheel (which was actually a primitive turbine, as can be seen from the illustration) was designed to provide power in situations where there was low water flow, and given the improvements that had been required in order to supply

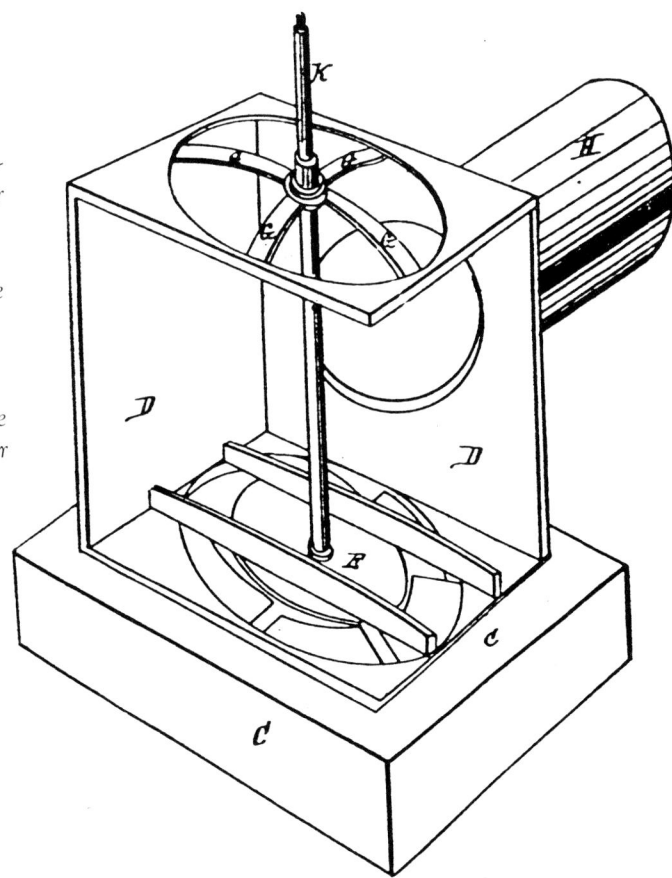

Barton and Alvin Darling's water wheel was actually a primitive turbine. This enlarged view of the patent drawing shows how the water from the trench (sometimes called a "flume") would arrive through the pipe on the right. It would then drive a propeller like wheel at the bottom. This was a huge improvement over earlier water wheels and was a revolutionary device in the 1830s.

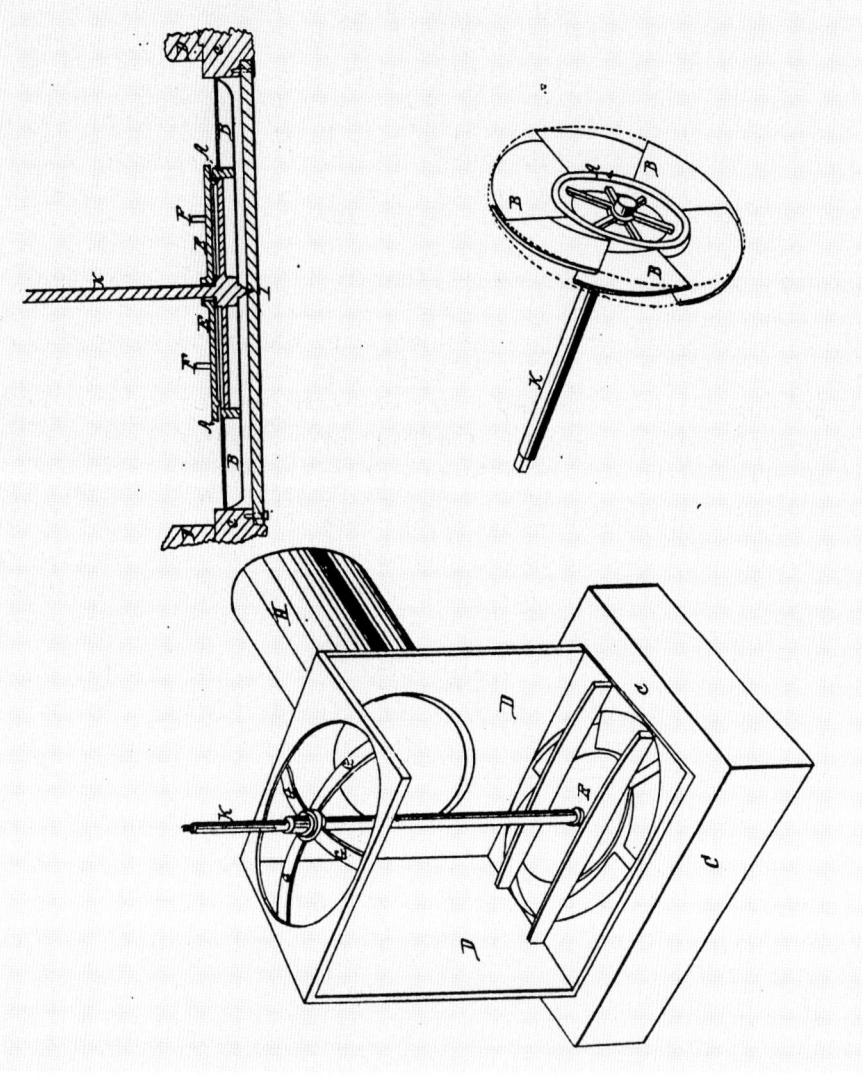

(right) The earliest version of the Woonsocket Patriot ad for Darlings' Spiral Pressure Wheel. This advertisement was much longer than what is shown here, including many endorsements from happy customers. These endorsements, called "Certificates," are reproduced on the following pages.

(left page) The patent drawings for the Darling water wheel. The description page appears to have been lost, doubtless in the Patent Office fire.

Spiral Pressure Wheels.

THE subscribers having lately obtained from the United States, letters patent for an improvement in Water Wheels which are adapted to all kinds of mills operated by water power, now offer for sale State, County or Town rights, as will best suit the convenience of purchasers. The Spiral Pressure Wheel is made of cast and wrought iron, and is so constructed as may easily be repaired, and is very little subject to get out of repair. One of the most important advantages of this wheel over any of the kind is, that the pressure of the column of water in the flume has no effect either on the arms of the wheel or the step; the wheel is therefore left free for the whole force or gravity of the water above it. It is very cheap, simple and durable. The subscribers are well aware of the prejudices existing among Mechanics and Manufacturers against many of the plans which have been put into operation under the name of *Reaction Wheels*, and while they would not detract from the merits of any of their competitors, they would respectfully invite a careful and candid examination of their recent invention, by those who are interested in the application of water power: this may be done by calling at their shop in Bellingham, or on *Jesse Whiting* at Woonsocket, or either of the gentlemen whose certificates are subjoined.

BARTON & ALVAN DARLING.
Bellingham, March 4, 1836.

their own shop with a reliable source of forceful water, this must have been a subject that was of immediate concern to the entire Darling family. Bungay Brook has a very low flow today, and from an inspection of the riverbed it does not seem that the situation was much different in historical times.

The Journal of the Franklin Institute made notes on all new patents and had this to say about the Darling Invention: "This is called

Certificates.

Hopkinton, Aug. 10, 1835.

This may certify that we have and are using the Patent Pressure Wheel made by Barton & Alvan Darling, and have applied one to a Saw Mill which fully answers our expectations. The benefit derived from the wheel is, it does not take half the quantity of water to saw one M. boards which the common kind of wheels require, and with much greater speed—and as far as we are acquainted with the use of the pressure wheel are satisfied that a great saving in the expense is made in the repairs. We have also applied one to a Grist Mill which answers equally as well as that in the saw mill, and we recommend them as well deserving the patronage of the public.

WILLIAM B. & ALBERT WOOD.

Bellingham, Aug. 12, 1835.

This is to certify that from November last to the present date I have made use of Messrs. B. & A. Darling's Spiral Pressure Water Wheel, one to drive a Grist Mill and one for a Saw Mill. I can now operate both saw and grist mill with drawing the same number of inches of water which it formerly took to drive the grist mill with breast float wheel 12 feet diameter, and with better speed.

DWIGHT COLBURN.

Bellingham, Sept. 1, 1835.

This may certify that I have operated a Saw Mill and Grist Mill about ten months, with A. & B. Darling's Spiral Pressure Wheels, under a variable head from two to eight feet. The wheels will run well, covered with thirty inches of flood water. I can do more business with half the quantity of water used with the old wheels. HENRY LILLIE.

Westminster, Oct. 16, 1835.

I hereby certify that I have had in use B. & A. Darling's Patent Pressure Water Wheel, for a Saw Mill and a Shingle Machine for some six months, and I find them as good as I expected, and the best in my opinion now in use.

WM. WISWALL.

Endorsements from the original Woonsocket Patriot ad for the Darlings's Spiral Pressure Wheel, continued next page.

Westminster, Oct. 19, 1835.

We hereby certify that we have had in use B. & A. Darling's Patent Water Wheel for a Shingle Machine for one year, and find it to answer a good purpose. PRESTON ELLIS, LIBERTY PARTRIDGE.

Westborough, Nov. 10, 1835.

This may certify that I have used one of B. & A. Darling's Patent Pressure Water Wheels in a Grist Mill for some months, and from the experience I have had, can say, that they are superior to any wheel now in use for me.

DANIEL CHAMBERLAIN.

Westborough, Nov. 18, 1835.

I hereby certify, that so far as I have been acquainted with B. & A. Darling's Cast Iron Wheel, which I have only made use of about three months with about eight feet head and fall. I can, with proper management,—grind from 10 to 12 bushels of old corn an hour, and other grain in proportion.

P. S. The cracker is connected with the maine shaft which always runs with the mill. Furthermore, the mill that formerly stood on the same head and fall, with a good tub wheel, would not grind more on an average, than five and a half or six bushels of grain in an hour.

JONATHAN PIKE.

Woonsocket Falls, March 1, 1836.

This may certify that I have used one of Messrs. B. & A. Darling's Wheels for the last three months, for operating a small Grinding and Polishing Shop. The head is about 6 feet, and the water power, from its location and other circumstances is subject to many disadvantages; I am however satisfied, that in point of cheapness, durability and power, it is unequaled by any wheel of the kind in this country. JESSE WHITING.

Woonsocket Falls, March 1, 1836.

This may certify that we have seen one of Messrs. B. & A. Darling's Spiral Pressure Wheels in operation in Mr. Jesse Whiting's grinding and finishing shop in this village, and are convinced

> that for cheapness of construction, durability and power, it is equal to any wheel of the kind used in this country, and performs beyond our expectation.
> THOMAS ARNOLD,
> DARIUS SIBLEY.
>
> *Caution.*
> All persons are hereby forbidden to use the cap of our wheel (which is patented) either in the form which we usually apply it or any other, by way of evasion, as all such trespasses will be legally noticed.
> 23).   B. & A. D.

The end of a long string of "Certificates" or endorsements that appeared below the original Woonsocket Patriot *ad for the Darlings's Spiral Pressure Wheel. All of these entries are testimonials from happy customers who have used the wheel and are recommending it to others. This was a common practice in 19th-century advertising and indeed is often seen today. Notice Barton and Alvin Darling's warning against infringement of their patent at the end.*

'The upright perpendicular pressure wheel, with spiral floats.' There is so little substantial difference between this and several of the wheels called reaction wheels, that we think it unnecessary to give any of the particulars of its construction; we could not, in fact, tell what the patentees view as constituting their improvement, as they have omitted altogether to communicate this important information."[17] The Darlings themselves went to pains to point out that the difference between their wheel and "Reaction Wheels" was in their wheel's cap, and that on their wheel "the pressure of the column of water has no effect either on the arms of the wheel or step; the wheel is therefore left free for the whole force or gravity of the water above it."

On March 4, 1836, Barton and Alvin began advertising in the *Woonsocket Patriot* newspaper that they had "lately obtained from the United States, letters patent for an improvement in Water Wheels…" This advertisement further elaborated that their "Spiral Pressure Wheel is made of cast and wrought iron" and that anyone interested in viewing it can do so "by calling at their shop in Bellingham, or on Jesse Whiting at Woonsocket." Whiting operated a small grinding and polishing shop and is one of many happy customers quoted in the ad, generally saying that they could do more work with less water flow than with their previous wheels. The Whitings, like the Darlings, were an old Bellingham family and their homestead is still standing on South Main Street.

The advertisement ran unchanged every week until late in 1836 when it was adjusted to suggest that customers call on "their shop in Bellingham, or on Alvan Darling, at Woonsocket." From this information, we learn that Alvin had moved to Woonsocket, while Barton remained behind at their old shop in Bellingham. Alvin's move to Woonsocket is confirmed by the appearance of his household in a news-

Spiral Pressure Wheels.

THE subscribers having lately obtained from the United States, letters patent for an improvement in Water Wheels which are adapted to all kinds of mills operated by water power, now offer for sale State, County or Town rights, as will best suit the convenience of purchasers. The Spiral Pressure Wheel is made of cast and wrought iron, and is so constructed as may easily be repaired, and is very little subject to get out of repair. One of the most important advantages of this wheel over any of the kind is, that the pressure of the column of water in the flume has no effect either on the arms of the wheel or the step; the wheel is therefore left free for the whole force or gravity of the water above it. It is very cheap simple and durable. The subscribers are well aware of the prejudices existing among Mechanics and Manufacturers against many of the plans which have been put into operation under the name of *Reaction Wheels*, and while they would not detract from the merits of any of their competitors, they would respectfully invite a careful and candid examination of their recent invention, by those who are interested in the application of water power; this may be done by calling at their shop in Bellingham, or on Alvan Darling, at Woonsocket, or either of the gentlemen whose certificates are subjoined.

BARTON & ALVAN DARLING.
Bellingham, March 4, 1836.

Caution.

All persons are hereby forbidden to use the cap of our wheel (which is patented) either in the form which we usually apply it or any other, by way of evasion, as all such trespasses will be legally noticed.
3) B. & A. D.

The final version of the Woonsocket Patriot ad for Darling's Spiral Pressure Wheel. Notice that at the bottom the text indicates that Alvin Darling has established a shop in Woonsocket.

paper listing of Woonsocket residents for 1836.[18] While the street address of Alvin's new shop in Woonsocket has not been discovered, it was across the river from the main village and alongside the Globe Manufacturing Company, near Globe Pond. This pond is filled in now, but it can be seen in old photographs and maps. Alvin took out a long

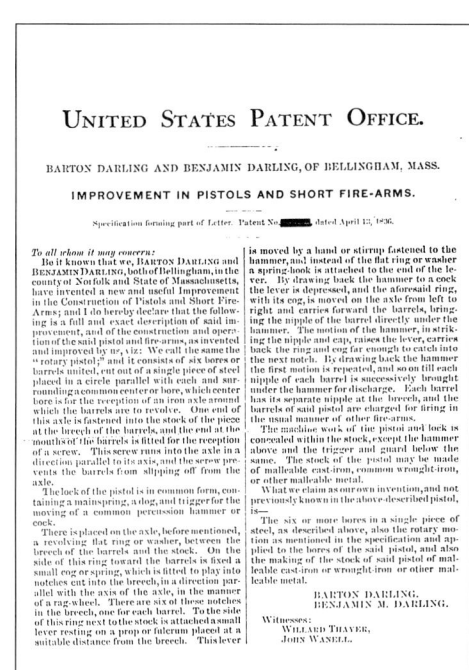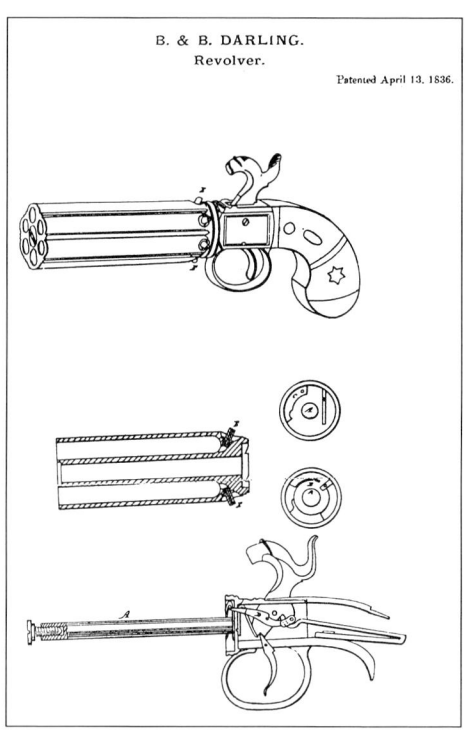

Small reproductions of the April 13, 1836, patent documents for the Darling pepperbox pistol. Larger versions of these illustrations will be shown later.

term lease for this land, including rights to the water power, and permission to erect buildings and a water wheel.[19] From the terms of later leases, we know that the buildings and water wheel were indeed erected. The revised water wheel advertisement ran through April 1837, when it was canceled and never resumed.

It is interesting that at about the same time that Barton and Alvin were patenting and manufacturing their water wheel, Barton and Benjamin M. were patenting and making early examples of another invention featuring some iron construction — the Darling pepperbox pistol. The brothers received their patent for an improvement in pistols and short fire-arms on April 13, 1836,[20] and from a comparison of the patent drawings to actual surviving pistols, it is quite clear that the drawings are based upon finished examples of the invention in its fully-developed form. There is nothing in the patent drawings that differs in style or substance from the guns as manufactured.

On September 18, 1837, Barton and Benjamin M. Darling displayed their pepperbox invention at an Exhibition and Fair of the

The Darling Pepperbox

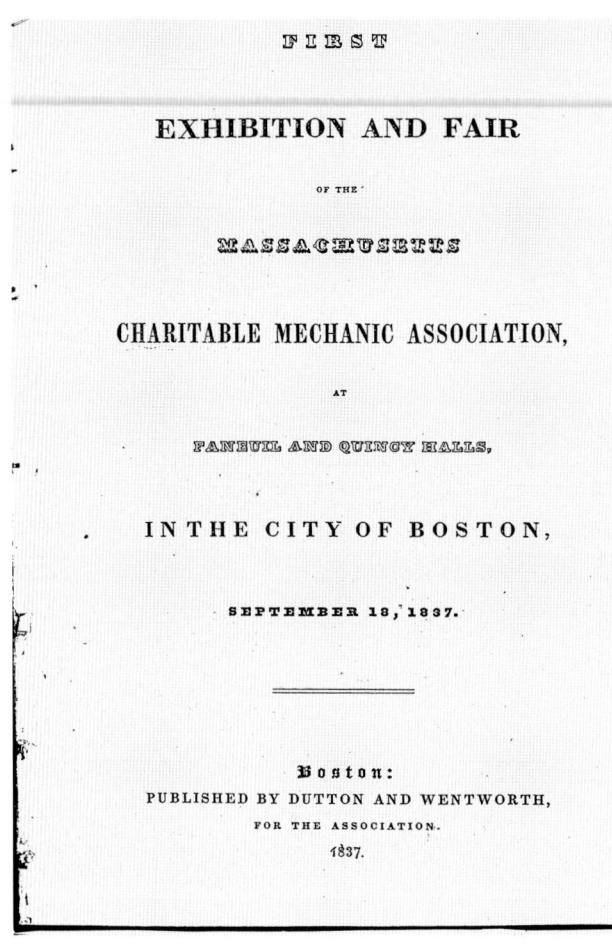

The title page of the catalog for the "First Exhibition and Fair of the Massachusetts Charitable Mechanic Association" published in 1837. The Darlings were awarded a diploma for their pepperbox pistol at this prestigious event. Other firearms makers displaying their innovations included: D.H. Chamberlain, S.B. Allen, E.A. Bennett, P.W. Whittier, Henry Pratt, James Eaton, B.T. Edmands, Isaac Davis, A. Waters, Morrill, Mossman and Blair, Andrews & Osborne, Cyrus Alger, N.P. Ames, Thomas W. Lyon, A. Clark, H.C. Fay, J.L. Clendennin, and Francis & Lovel. (Provided to the author through the courtesy of Nick Chandler)

Massachusetts Charitable Mechanic Association in Boston. The Association was founded in 1795 by Paul Revere. They began to hold exhibitions in 1837 and would continue to do so about every three years. The catalog of this event lists the Darlings in this way:

147. B. & B.M. Darling, Bellingham. A patent rotary Pistol, with six barrels, made from a solid piece of cast steel, which turn by the act of cocking. They are neat specimens of ingenuity and mechanical skill, well adapted for many uses.

The pepperbox was awarded a diploma for excellence.[21] The buildings where the exhibition was held, Faneuil Hall and Quincy Hall, remain famous Boston landmarks to this day and are top tourist attractions in that city. They are massive, prominent buildings in the center of

The Darling Pepperbox

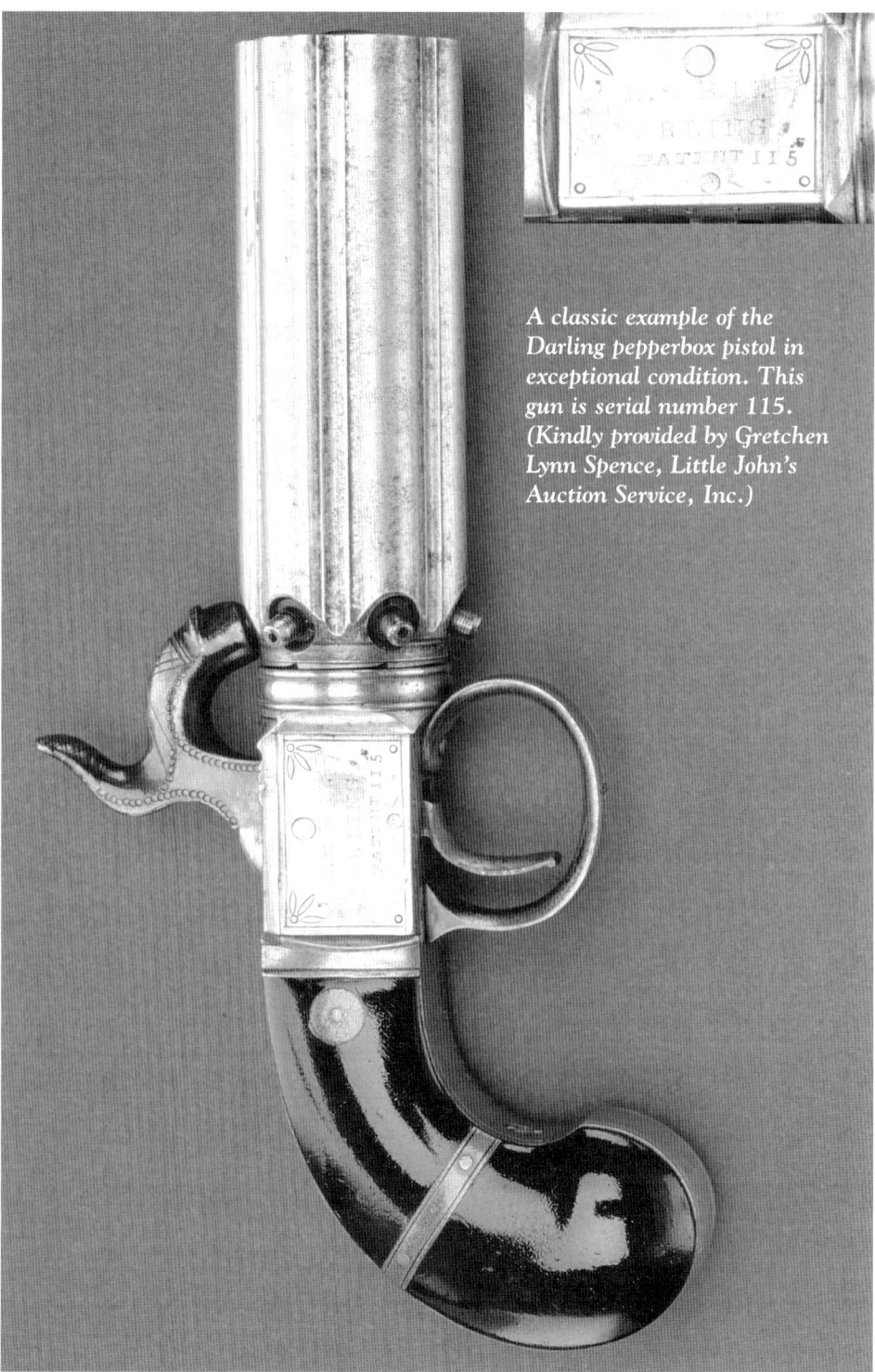

A classic example of the Darling pepperbox pistol in exceptional condition. This gun is serial number 115. (Kindly provided by Gretchen Lynn Spence, Little John's Auction Service, Inc.)

> 147. B. & B. M. DARLING, *Bellingham.* A patent rotary Pistol, with six barrels, made from a solid piece of cast steel, which turn by the act of cocking. They are neat specimens of ingenuity and mechanical skill, well adapted for many uses. *A Diploma.*

Entry for the Darling pepperbox in the catalog for the "First Exhibition and Fair of the Massachusetts Charitable Mechanic Association" published in 1837. The term "cast steel" above does not mean that the barrels were cast in a mold. Cast steel, also known as crucible steel, was a type of high carbon steel often used in the arms industry.

Boston's commercial district, and when the exhibition was held there they were connected by a temporary bridge. This event must have been an impressive show. These exhibitions were nationally renowned during the 19th century, and today many of the items that were shown at them are displayed in museums.

The compliments paid to the Darlings in the catalog should not be seen as polite trivialities. The descriptions for some of the other inventions, a number of which were for firearms innovations, were quite caustic, listing their faults and pointing out weaknesses in their design and manufacture. The Darlings had received a "rave review" from a tough critic at an important event. They must have been ecstatic.

On April 27, 1838, the brothers began advertising the pepperbox in their local newspaper, the *Woonsocket Patriot*. The advertisement read, "Darling's Patent Rotary Pistols, Made and Sold Wholesale and Retail by B. & B.M. Darling, Woonsocket, R.I." It was repeated in every single issue of the *Woonsocket Patriot* until March 15, 1839.

This advertisement raises an interesting question. Why do they list their address as Woonsocket? The Woonsocket address in the ads may indicate that they had a Woonsocket operation supplementing or replacing their mill in Bellingham. Their brother Alvin had already relocated there, so this does not seem entirely unlikely. Or perhaps this just indicates that they collected their mail at that particular post office. The Wrentham Road location was rural and many miles from Bellingham center. The Woonsocket post office was a good deal closer, and from newspaper listings of unclaimed letters we know that they did indeed receive their mail there.

Another thing to notice from the newspaper advertisement is that the word "wholesale" comes before the word "retail." As small mill operators, the Darlings would have had no way to sell many of their pistols direct to customers. They must have depended upon dealers and wholesalers to bring their goods to market.

DARLING'S PATENT ROTARY PISTOLS,
MADE AND SOLD WHOLESALE AND RETAIL BY
B. & B. M. DARLING
WOONSOCKET, R. I.

Advertisement for the Darling pepperbox. This ad appeared in every issue of the Woonsocket Patriot *from April 27, 1838 through March 15, 1839.*

One example of their pepperbox may shed light upon this part of their business operations. While almost all of the Darling pepperboxes are marked with the names of the Darlings themselves, this pistol is marked "W. GLAZE COLUMBIA, S.C. PATENT 4". William Glaze was a dealer in South Carolina who acted as a retailer and middle man for all sorts of hardware and fancy goods, although he had a special interest in firearms. It was normal practice for guns to be marked by the retailer rather than the original manufacturer, so seeing the name of a dealer like Glaze on a Darling gun is not surprising. Glaze is known to have put his name on all sorts of guns made by other men, and many of these firearms originated in the Northeast.[22]

The Glaze-marked Darling will be discussed more thoroughly later in this book. It is a challenging gun to assess and its configuration raises some serious questions. However, it remains an excellent reminder that the Darlings were looking to sell their guns through all the available outlets and not necessarily to the occasional visitor at their Bellingham mill.

It was mentioned above that the Darling pepperbox advertisements were discontinued after March 15, 1839. Why did they stop advertising? One piece of evidence that may help answer this question is a deed dated on March 28, 1839, in which Barton and his father sell nine acres, including all the buildings on that land and full water privileges, to their relatives Welcome and Almon Darling. While these early land records are hard to understand (they describe property according to long-gone landmarks such as trees and piles of stones), it appears that this land included the house on Wrentham Road and Barton's nearby pistol/machine shop.[23] If this is true, then the advertisements stopped just a few days before the pistol shop was sold, which would seem to make sense.

In any case, they definitely relocated to Woonsocket at this time and were no longer listed as residents of Bellingham when an important census was taken in early 1840.[24] After the sale of the Wrentham Road property, Barton and Benjamin M. purchased a piece of property from Waldo Earle, "in the village of Woonsocket...on the highway heading from the village to Mendon."[25] This deed, dated April 9, 1840, is the first legal document I have found that lists the Darling brothers as residents of Cumberland (which included Woonsocket). Since they purchased this land in partnership, and the price was quite high, we must assume that it was for business or investment use, although this is not a location known to have had water power. Whatever this land was intended for, it didn't last long because they sold the property at a substantial loss less than a year later.[26]

During this period, the Darlings definitely lived in Woonsocket proper and it is probable that Benjamin was living in Barton's home.[27] Not only are they included as Woonsocket residents in contemporary listings, but Barton also served on the Woonsocket School Committee for the years 1842 and 1843, having responsibility for educational expenditures in District 1, which included the "downtown" portion of Woonsocket between the main falls and the Social Mill. Again, this would confirm that he was living in the village of Woonsocket proper and not in one of its many surrounding neighborhoods.[28] It also shows that within just a couple of years of his arrival, Barton was already a respected and trusted member of the community.

In early 1842, the family's father, Benjamin Darling, passed away. Barton, as the eldest son, served as administrator and presumably inherited a significant portion of his estate. Aside from this loss, 1842 must have been a stressful year in the lives of the Darling family for other reasons, because it was also the year that Woonsocket and Bellingham were embroiled in the Dorr Rebellion.

The Dorr Rebellion (or Dorr War) was an armed uprising or civil war in Rhode Island that pitted the established political system (often referred to as the Law and Order Party) against a party of populists led by mill owner Thomas W. Dorr. Woonsocket (a mill town with many workers who were not allowed to vote) was the major Dorrite strong-

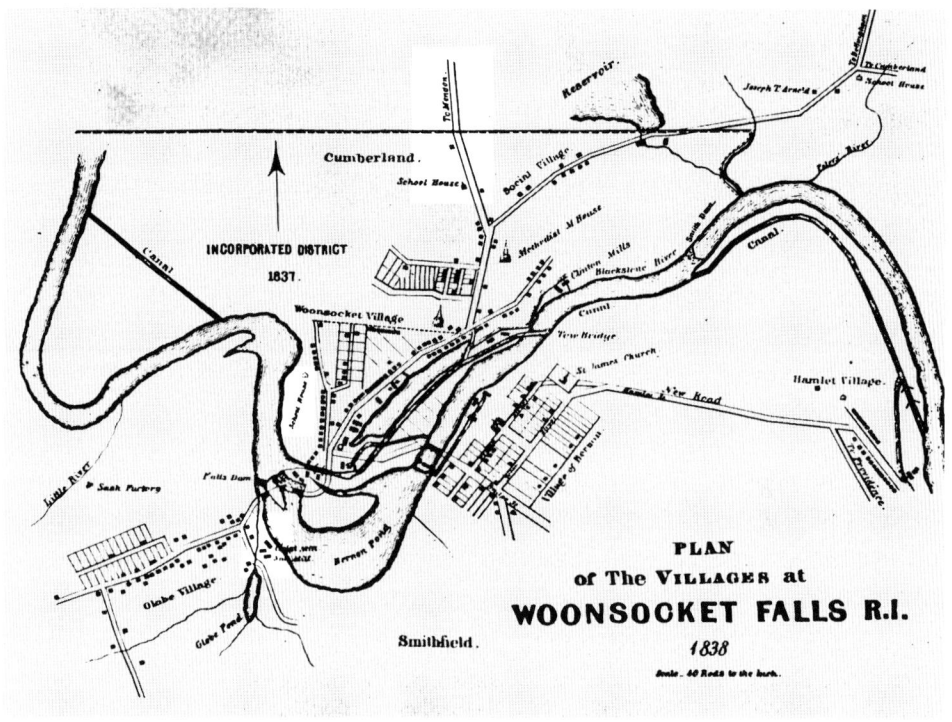

A detailed street map for Woonsocket Falls, drawn in 1838. Three areas of this map have been highlighted in white. The top white area shows where Barton and Benjamin M. Darling purchased land from Waldo Earle on the highway to Mendon. The center white area shows the school that Barton Darling was responsible for as part of his duties on the Woonsocket School Committee. The bottom white area shows the location of Alvin Darling's leased mill in the Globe neighborhood of Woonsocket, which was actually across the river in the town of Smithfield.

hold. Several well-advertised and festive clam bakes were held near the Cold Spring on Harris Avenue in order to raise money for the rebellion. After the end of hostilities, the city was occupied for two weeks under martial law by two hundred state troops.

According to some contemporary sources, the conflict also spilled over into Bellingham when the Dorrites raided that town, advancing as far as Crooks' Tavern (a drinking establishment less than a half mile down the road to the west of the original Darling pistol factory on the spot now occupied by "The Beverley" banquet hall). The Dorrite advance reportedly was halted at the tavern not by government troops but because their revolutionary activities were limited to terrorizing the barmaids and drinking all the rum before withdrawing back over the border.

This depiction of the Bellingham "raid," however, appears to be based upon false, politically motivated sources. The truth is that Bellingham, like Woonsocket, was strongly in the Dorrite camp and many Massachusetts residents from this community were active in Rhode Island politics and even voted in Rhode Island elections. Crooks' Tavern, being in a strong Dorrite neighborhood safely over the border in Massachusetts jurisdiction, became a staging ground for Dorrites and the site of many of their meetings. The tavern was raided by Rhode Island troops on June 30 and several rebels were taken back in custody. Two Rhode Island officers were later sued by the State of Massachusetts for their role in this incident.

Given that this hotbed of Dorrite activity was less then a half mile from his birthplace, it should not surprise us that Benjamin M. Darling played a crucial part in the action when the Dorrites invaded Rhode Island's capital city of Providence and turned captured cannon upon the assembled government troops. An excerpt from the *History of Providence County*, an 1891 oral history of Northern Rhode Island, reports this incident, as well as other details about the Darling family:

Members of the Darling family were also gifted with mechanical skill. It is claimed that the honor of inventing the revolving pistol, which has immortalized Colonel Colt, should belong to Barton Darling, who, with his brother Benjamin, had a shop in these parts where he had manufactured that article some time before the Colt revolver was produced. It is said of Benjamin Darling that he was an active adherent of Thomas W. Dorr, and that his bravery and determination prevented bloodshed at the most critical period of those troublous times. After the Dorrites had taken the cannon from the state arsenal, those holding them threatened to fire upon whoever should attempt to recapture them. A party of the "Law and Order" party advanced upon one of the cannons for this purpose, when just as the "Dorrites" were about to discharge the gun, Benjamin Darling rushed through the crowd and called upon it to desist, saying that such an act would be treason to the state, etc. To prevent firing he placed his hand on the vent, and kept it there even after the excited cannoneers had passed the heated priming rod over it and painfully burned it. His coolness produced better counsels and the peace was preserved, but not without leaving the stigma of traitor upon the heroic man. The Darlings invented other useful articles, but failed to reap pecuniary benefit from them, and Benjamin lived to become, in his extreme age, an object of the town's charity.[29]

Barton Darling's obituary in the Woonsocket newspaper. His entry is the second one down. Barton appears to have been the leader of his family's manufacturing ventures and his death had distressing financial consequences.

> **DIED.**
>
> In this Village, the 29th ult., Mrs. Priscilla, wife of Dr. Horatio Stockbridge, aged 63 years.
>
> The sickness of Mrs. S. was very brief, and until a short time previous to its termination, was not viewed as fatal. Hers was a quiet life; but it has left a fragrance that will not soon depart. She has left a husband to "sit and grieve alone," in the evening of his days, and to mourn that no answering voice comes back to him, when in bitterness of spirit, he yearns for the sympathy of the long tried and devoted companion. But he sorrows not as those who have no hope, and thus, in his vision, "beauty immortal awakes from the tomb." Two children, and an aged mother who had doted on her as the staff of her declining years, with many other relatives are mourners with him, and we trustingly commend them all to the Supreme and universal Father, as an unchanging Friend and Benefactor. B.
>
> [Providence and Boston papers please copy.]
>
> In this Village, the 6th inst., Mr. Barton Darling. Long and painful has been his sickness; but he suffered patiently, and died, trusting in God as his Friend, and the Savior of all men. He has left a wife, two brothers and a sister to sorrow for his absence, yet eo rejoice in his deliverance, since disease had made life a burden. Peace be with them. B.

While Benjamin M. was being labeled as a traitor by his neighbors, Barton appears to have begun a long struggle with some sort of chronic and fatal illness. On July 25, 1844, he purchased a burial plot for himself, which shows just how serious this sickness must have been.[30] Barton struggled on until his death on July 6, 1848. His obituary in the *Woonsocket Patriot* read, "died...in this village, the 6th inst., Mr. Barton Darling. Long and painful has been his sickness; but he suffered patiently, and died, trusting in God as his Friend, and the Savior of all men. He has left a wife, two brothers and a sister to sorrow for his absence, yet to rejoice in his deliverance, since disease had made life a burden. Peace be with them."

Barton's brother Benjamin M. was named administrator of his estate. After an examination of Barton's assets, which totaled $226.12.5, it was decided that the "estate is insolvent and insufficient to pay the just debts which said Barton owed at the time of his decease."[31] As an act of charity, the probate court allowed Barton's widow Persis to keep her furniture, domestic items and other possessions that were considered "necessary for the upholding of life." Amongst the items liquidated to partially satisfy creditors were a gun valued at eight dollars, a smaller gun valued at two dollars, a rifle valued at twelve dollars, a lot of carpenter's tools, a smith's vice, a rifling machine and other tools.

The estate inventory for Barton Darling is interesting in that it contains a detailed list of the manufacturing equipment that he owned in partnership with his brother Benjamin M.[32] This list is quite extensive and shows that the Darlings were equipped to manufacture all the parts of their pepperboxes — even the complex solid barrel clusters that were the hardest part of the job. The organization of the tools into numbered drawers might suggest that they still had a working shop at this time, although this does not necessarily prove that the pistols themselves were still in actual production.

Personal property belonging to B. & B.M. Darling, September 2nd, 1848

Drawer #1	Files		4.00
Drawer #2	Brace & Bits		3.00
Drawer #3	Files		5.00
Drawer #4	Jamb Plate & Taps		5.00
Drawer #5	Sundries		.50
Drawer #6	Screws & Nails		.50
Drawer #7	[no description]		3.00

1 Box & Contents,	2.00	
Copper Kettle & contents,	2.25	4.25
1 pr Tinmans Shears,	3.00	
Types,	2.50	5.50
Shot & Lead,	1.00	
Lot of old trumpery,	4.00	5.00
1 Smith's Anvil,	10.08	
one vice,	2.00	12.08
1 Turning engine		45.00
1 Turning Lathe		15.00
12 prs. hand screws		3.00
2 Smith's vices,	3.00	
Blacksmith's Tools,	3.00	6.00
Arbours & Reams,	2.00	
Anvil & Iron,	2.00	4.00
Files, Lathe Buff Wheel & Lathing Engine		4.00
Grindstone,	4.00	
Upright drilling Lathe,	6.00	10.00
Fluting Engine,	1.00	
one work bench,	1.50	2.50
1 Ash Plank, 80ft.		2.40

Total	*$139.73*
Deduct 1/2 belonging to B.M. Darling	*$69.86.5*

    The careful reader will have noticed that the Woonsocket location of the pepperbox mill where these tools were used has not been identified. This is not in order to create drama, but because the answer is not conclusively known. No records yet discovered give a specific address and there was no real estate listed in Barton's probate records. Perhaps they simply rented work space in downtown Woonsocket near where they lived, because an exhaustive examination of deeds has failed to show that they owned manufacturing property of their own. A simpler answer might be that the pepperbox operation had failed and was discontinued in 1839 when the advertisements stopped and the mill in Bellingham was closed. Perhaps no pistols were made in Woonsocket at all and Woonsocket was just an address that they had used for advertising purposes. Given the small number of pistols produced, this is an entirely valid possibility.

    However, an intriguing additional possibility remains. Remember that their brother Alvin Darling had leased land in the Globe neighborhood, across the river from Woonsocket proper, back in October of 1836 with the term of the lease to begin on April 1, 1837. This is when the advertisements for the water wheel were discontinued, probably signalling that the lease was for another enterprise entirely. Well, this date is right between when the pepperbox was patented and when it was shown in Boston at the mechanical fair. Advertisements for the pepperbox begin appearing in 1837 with the address listed as Woonsocket, and it does not seem ridiculous that the three Darling brothers might have been reunited under one roof on Alvin's leasehold.

    One tantalizing piece of evidence about possible Woonsocket pepperbox production is an advertisement by the prominent and influential New York City arms importer and dealer A.W. Spies. This advertisement shows a percussion pepperbox with a cocked hammer that looks very much like a Darling. It is shown across from an Allen pepperbox, and the advertisement's address shows that it dates to 1846–1848, the last two years of Barton's life.[33] However, it would be easy to make too much of this evidence. Although I am quite sure that it depicts a Darling, the woodcut in question is far from detailed and is perhaps open to other interpretations. Also, there is no reason to think that Spies did not have an old Darling that was chosen as a model for this particular illustration,

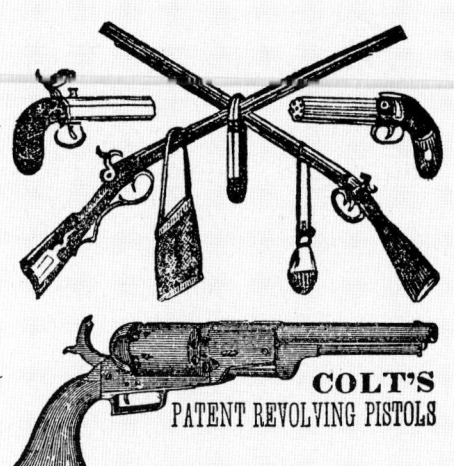

An advertisement for A.W. Spies & Co. From the address we know that it dates from c.1846–1848. Notice what appears to be a Darling pepperbox to the left of the crossed rifles at the top. (From *Ethan Allen, Gunmaker,* by Harold R. Mouillesseaux, published by Museum Restoration Service)

or that the woodcut itself was dated at the time that this advertisement was printed. Despite these concerns, when added to the tools and materials in Barton's probate list, this Spies advertisement remains the most compelling basis for an argument that Darling pepperboxes were manufactured after the brothers had moved from Bellingham to Woonsocket.

This possibility is reinforced by the fact that Alvin terminated his lease "forever" on June 6, 1848, exactly one month before Barton died and when it must have been clear that the pepperbox venture would have to be dissolved. That's a pretty big coincidence, and for this reason Alvin's mill in Globe is currently the best candidate for the pepperbox factory's possible Woonsocket location.[34]

However, I think that it would be a mistake to imply that pistols were all that were made there, or even that they were the primary product. Alvin must have been doing something else on his property, perhaps with the part-time help of his brothers, because the total number of pistols manufactured and sold would never have been enough to support even one workman for the number of years that the mill was in operation. It seems quite possible that only a few pistols were made in Woonsocket and that the brothers were focusing on other ventures following the 1839 sale of their Bellingham pistol mill.

Unfortunately, like so many of the other properties key to the Darling story, the deeds and other land records for Alvin's mill in the Globe section of Woonsocket offer descriptions that are less than helpful in locating an exact address. Alvin's leased mill site is described as "Beginning at a stake and stones on the line of land belonging to the Globe Manufacturing Company thence running southwesterly with said company's land ten rods thence westerly about fifteen rods in a line that shall intersect the land belonging to the heirs of John J. Paine...bound together with the water power to the same belonging."[35] From existing contracts, we know that he erected buildings and a mill powered by a water wheel, but I can only place the property to within the third of a square mile that is shown on the map at right. This is blown up from a larger map, already shown on page 37.

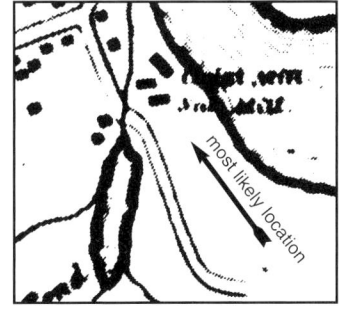

Barton's death must have been quite a disaster to the Darling family, and to his partner/brother in particular. Whether Benjamin M. continued in the gunsmithing business after his brother's death is unknown, although it appears from the paperwork that the pistol making tools were liquidated in order to satisfy claims on Barton's estate. Presumably, Benjamin M. did not have the money or inclination to buy back Barton's half of the partnership, and with Alvin's mill gone with the canceled lease, things must have seemed pretty grim indeed.

Perhaps as a reflection of his reduced circumstances, by 1857 Benjamin M. had taken residence at an inexpensive boarding house called the Mechanic's Hotel on Main Street in Woonsocket. In directories, he was listing himself as a machinist. Operated by Albert Jencks and later Lysander Elliott, the Mechanic's Hotel was a structure 42x110 feet, three stories high and surmounted by a Mansard story.[36] Woonsocket's industry was growing leaps and bounds at this time, and whether he was working for himself or others there must have been some amount of employment for a man of his skills.

From 1869 to 1872, city directories show him as a machinist boarding in a house at 73 Arnold Street, near the corner of Fountain Street, in Woonsocket.[37] Benjamin M. Darling was still an active inventor during this period, because on January 11, 1869 he received U.S. Patent #86,141 for an "Improved Seat for Chairs, Cars, &c." In his application, he claimed that the "invention consists in a novel construction of a chair, car, or other seat, in combination with the frame on which it is supported, whereby the seat is rendered movable thereon, without becoming detached, and susceptible of adjustment, either in a more or less inclined plane with reference to the frame on which it rests or is supported." In other words, Benjamin M. invented a "Lay-Z-Boy"-style, wooden recliner that could also be used as the driver's seat of a horse-drawn carriage.

In 1880 and 1881, the *Woonsocket Directory* lists him as a farmer living in a house on "Diamond Hill Road, beyond Mendon Road." This location is part of the land previously owned by his father and grandfather along the border with Bellingham and is on a road running parallel with the Wrentham Road where his Bellingham pistol factory had been. From city directories, it can be seen that his house was right next to Darling Pond, which can be found on the map (see page 47).[38] This address is listed for many members of the Darling extended family, and a number of households seem to have lived there together, perhaps in a cluster or string of houses along the road. It is clear from the Directories that many of the Darlings at this address (and elsewhere in the city, for that matter) were either machinists or gunsmiths.[39]

B. M. DARLING.
SEAT FOR CHAIRS, CARS, &c.

No. 86,141. Patented Jan. 26, 1869.

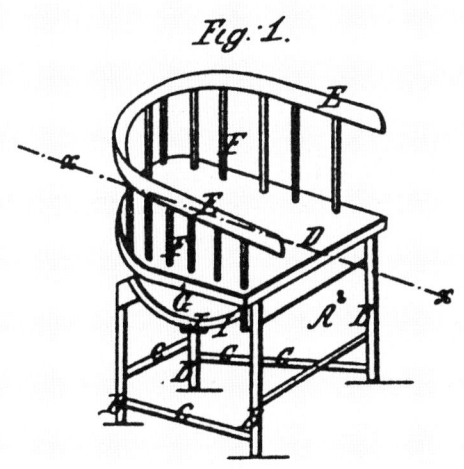

Fig. 1.

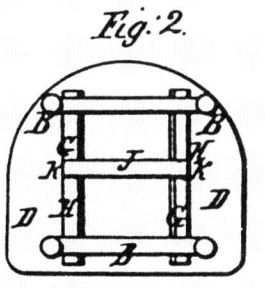

Fig. 2.

Fig. 3.

Witnesses;
Albert W. Brown
H. L. Wattenberg

Inventor;
B. M. Darling

BENJAMIN M. DARLING, OF WOONSOCKET, RHODE ISLAND.

Letters Patent No. 86,141, dated January 26, 1869; antedated January 11, 1869.

IMPROVED SEAT FOR CHAIRS, CARS, &c.

The Schedule referred to in these Letters Patent and making part of the same.

To all whom it may concern:

Be it known that I, BENJAMIN M. DARLING, of Woonsocket, in the county of Providence, and State of Rhode Island, have invented a new and useful Improvement in Seats for Chairs, Cars, &c.; and I do hereby declare that the following is a full, clear, and exact description thereof, which will enable others skilled in the art to make and use the same, reference being had to the accompanying drawings, forming part of this specification.

The present invention consists in a novel construction of a chair, car, or other seat, in combination with the frame on which it is supported, whereby the seat is rendered movable thereon, without becoming detached, and susceptible of adjustment, either in a more or less inclined plane with reference to the frame on which it rests or is supported.

In the accompanying plate of drawings my improvement in seats for chairs, cars, &c., is illustrated—

Figure 1 being a perspective view of a chair having its seat and supporting-frame constructed according thereto;

Figure 2, a plan view of the under side to a chair-seat; and

Figure 3, a vertical section, taken in the plane of the line x x, fig. 1.

A, in the drawings, represents the supporting framework to a chair, consisting of legs B, joined together by rounds C at suitable points.

D, the seat, having a continuous rail, E, supported by upright posts or rounds, F, at suitable points.

This rail E forms a rest for the back and the arms of the person sitting in the chair.

To the under side of the chair-seat two ribs, G, are applied or attached, extending from front to rear in parallel lines.

These ribs, upon their under sides H, are made of a convex circular or arc-shape, and by such sides rest and bear upon similar concave circular or arc-shape ribs or bars I, secured to the supporting-frame A, at its upper end, in proper position therefor.

J, a cross-bar or rail, connecting the two convex ribs, G, of chair-seat together, and extending, by its ends K, under the bars I, whereby the seat D is confined to the supporting-frame A, this bar J, at the same time, however, offering no obstruction to the free motion of the seat over the concave bars or ribs I from front to rear.

From the above description of the combined construction of the chair-frame A, and its seat B, it is obvious that, without the seat becoming detached from its supporting-frame, it can be inclined at an angle more or less great with regard thereto, according as may be desired by the person seated therein, to produce the necessary comfort and ease.

And it may be here observed that, if so desired, a foot-rest may be arranged in connection with the seat, so as to have a corresponding motion therewith.

And, furthermore, that although I have described my invention more particularly in connection with chair-seats, it may be applied as well to car and other seats; and therefore I do not intend to limit myself in its use to any one particular form or kind of seat.

Having thus described my improvement,

What I claim as my invention, is—

The convex ribs G, applied to seat D, and provided with a cross-bar, J, in combination with the concave ribs or bars I, fixed to supporting-frame A, substantially as and for the purpose described.

BENJAMIN M. DARLING.

Witnesses:
J. P. POND,
HERBERT F. HEITH.

Benjamin M. Darling's patent description for a reclining chair that could also be used on horse drawn carriages. The drawings for this patent appear on the previous page.

The Darling Pepperbox

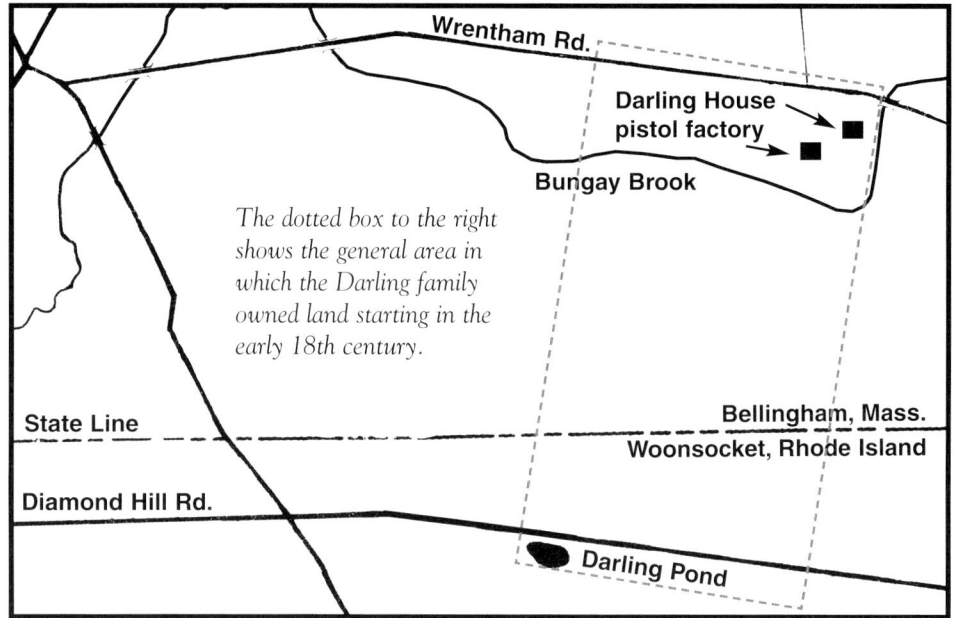

This map shows Benjamin M. Darling's "Darling Pond" where he lived on Diamond Hill Road and his birthplace on Wrentham Road. The distance between the two sites is .7 miles. The Darling family had owned a patchwork of farm land in this area since at least the 1720s with each and every generation being metalworkers. Given the acreage involved, it is probably safe to assume that they were farmers as well. This area has rich soil, but it is also a glacial spill zone. It was a popular joke in the old days that they spent most of their time farming rocks. The stone walls found throughout this region are silent testimony to the bitter truth of this jest.

Benjamin M. Darling was over seventy years old and living in poverty.[40] Luckily, Woonsocket had an effective, flexible approach to poor relief and Darling's case is a good example. While he seems to have owned a farm, no tax was collected, probably because of his reduced circumstances. In 1882, he began to receive direct relief from the city's Overseer of the Poor. Being too old to work, he moved away from the Diamond Hill Road farm and was given subsidized rent to live in an apartment. Over the next few years he received substantial help from the city, including rent, supplies, cash and food.[41] In 1884, he is listed at 46 Coe Street, which was in a sparsely settled area quite close to the City Asylum for the Poor. In 1886, he made another short move to 26 Coe Street, where he is listed as a boarder. Other houses on Coe Street were owned by Darlings and it seems likely that he was either living with relatives or boarding near their homes so that they could take care of him.[42]

The Darling Pepperbox

Benjamin M. Darling's obituary.

The City Asylum for the Poor as it looks today. Benjamin M. Darling died here. The property is still owned by the City of Woonsocket. The fields are used for sports and recreation, and the building continues in its original spirit, helping those who are in need of care.

Finally, sometime after April 30, 1888, he was moved to the City Asylum for the Poor, where he received direct care. The Asylum was a large, working farm that housed about a dozen very old or very poor residents. The younger residents worked in the fields and sold any surplus crops at market. It is interesting that there were enough surplus crops not only to support the Asylum, but also to pay for all other forms of poor relief in the town with a bit left over. A 1910 photo of the Asylum or "Poor Farm House" shows a massive home with a big porch in front, a picket fence, a large barn and a third smaller building. Everything looks quite well tended.

Benjamin M. Darling died at the City Asylum on April 7, 1890. He was 82 years of age, and since there were no doctors called to the Asylum during his last months, it does not seem that he suffered a long illness. A funeral service was held for him at the Asylum, and he was buried at an unknown location — perhaps on the Asylum's grounds in a "potter's field."

A Visit to the Darling Pistol Factory

Despite the fact that I live in Woonsocket and have easy access to all the local archives and record vaults, it took me almost a year of on-and-off research to confirm the location where Darling pepperboxes were made. This was accomplished through three documents described earlier. The first was an 1833 deed, in which Barton Darling purchased a dam site for his shop from a neighbor, Ichabod Chilson. The second was an original 1830 map of Bellingham, showing the homes of the Darlings, Ichabod Chilson, and the brook upon which the Darling shop was located. The third was a map, shown on page 22 of this book and dating to 1858, which depicts the dam and trench that Barton Darling constructed to power his mill.

One Saturday morning, with the deed and maps in hand, I headed out with my friend Joe Puleo to search for the Darling shop site. We quickly located Bungay Brook where it crossed Wrentham Road, and began to look for signs of the Darling homestead. The brook isn't very impressive today, and certainly wouldn't have provided much power to a mill during the 1800s. It is no wonder that Barton Darling's first invention was a water wheel especially designed to operate with limited water flow! Barton's eventual fix for this situation (the reservoir, dam and trench) were not to be seen.

None of the houses in the area looked particularly old, which was discouraging, but we headed down one of the long driveways on the south side of the road, hoping to ask if there were any old foundations in the area. We came to a nice house with a barn and horse corrals, and were ringing the doorbell when a man in a pickup truck drove up. We asked him about the foundations, and showed him our old map. He quickly answered that we were actually at the original Darling house, which had been substantially updated over the years. He also told us that the original owner had been a gunsmith who invented a fancy pepperbox. To think that I had spent all those hours trying to learn something that is apparently common knowledge in the neighborhood!

(above) A view of the Darling house from the rear. The current owner, concerned about his privacy, asked us not to photograph the house from the front and we respected his wishes. As can be seen, the house has seen significant remodeling and probably enlargement since the Darlings lived there.

(right) The view from the site of the pistol factory. Even today this location is quite rural and would probably still be familiar to the pistol-inventing men who lived and worked there.

The gentleman was very helpful, pointing out that Ichabod Chilson's house was still standing, too, and giving us directions. When asked about a shop or factory, he directed us to the "rake factory" — an old foundation that was used decades ago as an impromptu garbage dump. This section of Bellingham, once known as Mechanicsville, is now called Rakeville after this factory where a Mr. Jerald D. Wilcox made rakes and other agricultural implements. We

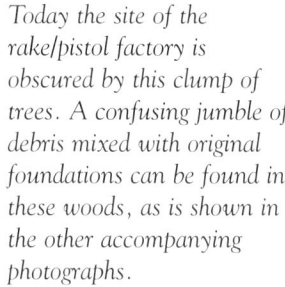

Today the site of the rake/pistol factory is obscured by this clump of trees. A confusing jumble of debris mixed with original foundations can be found in these woods, as is shown in the other accompanying photographs.

found the "rake factory" on a hillside near the brook, just 100 yards from the Darling house. Filled with a collapsed roof and assorted junk, the foundations were made of piled rocks in some places, and blocks of solid granite in others, seemingly indicating two or more generations of construction. It seemed of the proper age and location to have been a possible Darling workshop (previous to its use as a rake factory, of course).

While property records are vague and no map exists with the pistol shop named as such, there are reasons to think that the pistol factory and rake factory occupied approximately the same spot. Both early maps that post-date the creation of the trench and pistol factory are from after the pistol factory had been sold. The first, dated 1858, shows two manufacturing facilities

Partial stone foundations at the rake/pistol factory site in Bellingham. The area is so very overgrown that no pattern or sense could be made of what remains, although much of it must certainly be debris from the rake factory building that burned in 1905. Separating these ruins from any surviving portions of earlier Darling construction would be difficult indeed.

on the trench: the "J. Burlingame Argicultural Implement Manufactory" and "Wilcox & Darling." Notice that the Burlingame factory is not beside the running water, but directly on top of it, as if to indicate that the mill was straddled over the trench. This was a normal building method for mills in the area with the water commonly running right through the mill's basement.

The second map, dated 1876, identifies the mill as the "Rake Mfy." and the owner as "J.D. Wilcox." A residence for A. Darling is shown exactly where Benjamin and his pistol-inventing sons had lived.

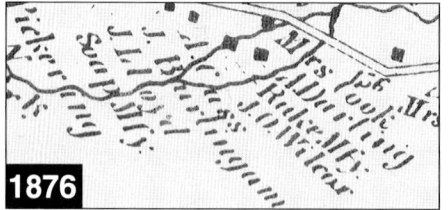

Remember that Benjamin and Barton sold their house and mill to Almon Darling in 1839. It seems likely that Almon Darling, who did not die until June of 1877, is the person shown on the 1876 map as owner of the house and on the 1858 map as partner in the Wilcox mill. J.D. Wilcox became famous as the owner of the rake factory, so it would seem that he was in partnership with Almon Darling in 1858 and operating in the pistol factory Almon had purchased in 1839.

Notice that the Burlingame factory shown on the 1858 map does not appear on the 1876 map, and was perhaps swallowed up by the expanding Wilcox operation, which would grow to employ about thirty people. This would explain why there are multiple generations of foundations on this site and leads me to believe that the rake factory was built on the general location of the pistol factory or was an expansion of

A cabinet card photograph of the Jerald D. Wilcox rake factory, which was destroyed by fire in 1905. This is the factory that gave "Rakeville" its name. This was either built on the foundations of, or next to, the Darling pistol factory. Some have even suggested that this building is the pistol factory itself. (Image courtesy of Fran Donovan)

it. My feeling is that we have found the foundations of the pistol factory, but that they are simply too mixed in with other construction and accumulated trash to make sense of them.[43]

We next went looking for the dam and trench opening on the north side of the road. Early maps show the trench beginning some distance northeast of the road. The dam is shown as a small rectangle. The brook up there is a wide swamp with no easy access and no stream leading off where the trench must have been. Doubtless this swamp was the reservoir that Barton created above the dam, but we could find no clear evidence of an old dam or trench. Eventually, we ended up hiking about

The Darling Pepperbox

Satellite views of the Darling homestead. Bungay Brook can be seen curving its way west. The Darling house is circled, an arrow points to the clump of trees where the pistol factory was, and a line has been drawn to show the general route of the pistol mill's trench.

1/2 of a mile through a farm field to approach the brook from the north. We found what appeared to be the brook's original bed, and then spent about two hours hiking through the swamp in search of a dam or trench site, or anything that looked like old construction.

Unfortunately, this area is horribly overgrown, and the ruins of an entire Roman city could have been hidden there without us finding it. All we "discovered" was a bad case of poison ivy. According to the old maps, however, the trench cut through what is now a housing development and crossed the road directly above the rake factory at a slight bend in the road near what is now the intersection with Lake Street. We found some stonework on the south side of the road above the rake factory site (next to a present-day machine shop), which might have been part of the trench system as it crossed the road, but with no additional evidence it is difficult to say. It did cross in that approximate area, though, because the terrain quickly turns uphill, which would not have allowed for practical trench construction.

Heading up Lake Street, we came across a historical cemetery. Amongst the many graves of 19th century residents were those of Ichabod Chilson (who sold Barton Darling the dam site) and Almon Darling, who purchased the pistol mill from Barton and his father in 1839 when they moved to Woonsocket.

The Darling Pepperbox

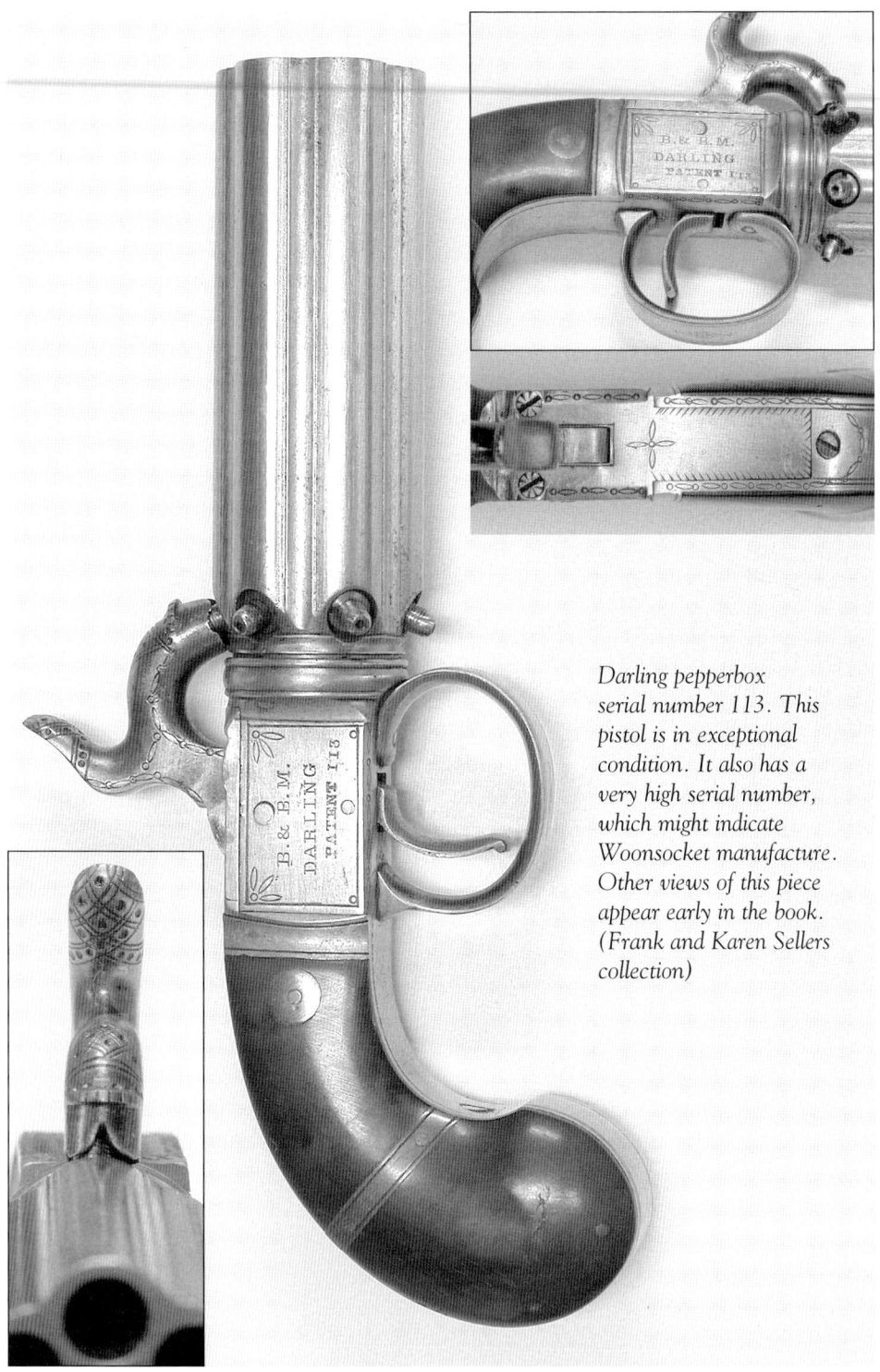

Darling pepperbox serial number 113. This pistol is in exceptional condition. It also has a very high serial number, which might indicate Woonsocket manufacture. Other views of this piece appear early in the book. (Frank and Karen Sellers collection)

The Pistols

Even today, many firearms collectors are confused about how to identify a true Darling pepperbox. They are, after all, quite rare and there are some vaguely similar European pistols that muddy the waters. This problem was even worse for earlier generations of arms historians. For example, in a January 1942 issue of *Gun Report*, Sam E. Smith wrote an entire article on Darlings, showing and describing eight examples, *none of which were actually Darling pepperboxes*. In all fairness, Smith had seen a photograph of a true Darling pepperbox, which he called the "first model" Darling, but had not been able to view or handle one himself.[44]

The non-Darlings that Smith illustrated and described were brass, hand rotated pistols with a vague similarity in shape to the true Darlings. Smith called these the "second model," guessing that after the original Darling venture failed they had turned to this cheaper version. These brass pistols, which Smith believed represented 98% of the total Darling output, were described specifically as Woonsocket production. However, all of these pistols were, in fact, Swedish pistols with no relationship to the Darling pepperbox at all. Smith's stature in the gun collecting world was such that these Swedish pistols were identified as Darlings in articles and books for decades, leaving even many advanced collectors in confusion to this day. All this was despite the fact that Smith corrected his mistake in 1966 after testing the wood from the grips of the brass pistols at the United States Forest Products lab and determining that the wood was from Northern Europe. Later correspondence with Swedish gun researchers would confirm for Smith that none of the brass guns were American at all.[45]

However, as is often the case, the original story proved much more resilient than the updated one, perhaps because the brass "Darlings" had been selling at a huge premium for years and collectors did not want to admit that what they had splurged for was really a cheap European gun with little American interest.[46] This situation was not helped by the fact that the Darling pistols most often illustrated in the American gun press during the last generation were those from the Harold's Club collection in Las Vegas, catalog numbers H96 and H97. But these, like those in the

The Darling Pepperbox

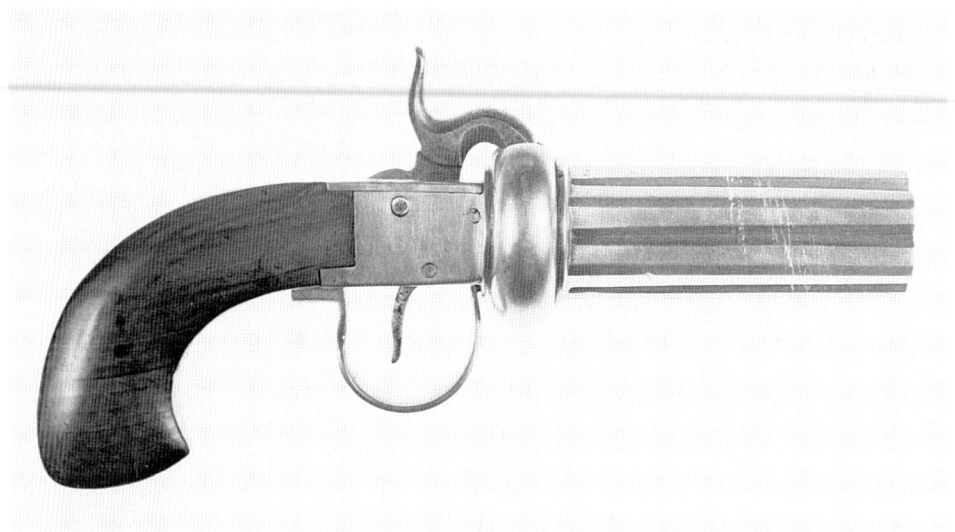

A Swedish "Darling" pepperbox marked "AGS". This marking stands for Anders Gustafsson, who worked for Engholm and later married his employer's daughter Johanna in 1869. The pistol is six shot, 27 caliber, and has a barrel group that measures 3-3/16". Readers interested in seeing further examples of these Swedish pistols, which exist in great variety, should refer to the 1973 book The William M. Locke Collection *with descriptions by Frank M. Sellers. (Courtesy of Robert Berryman)*

Smith article, were actually Swedish pistols of a similar general form but which had to be rotated by hand.

Even those authors today who understand that the brass versions are Swedish have often referred to early "hand rotated" Darlings, but to my knowledge these have always been broken pistols that are no longer operating properly, as can quickly be determined by disassembly of the pistol in question. I am aware of no evidence that there are any Darling pepperboxes meant to rotate by hand.

Since these Swedish pepperboxes have so often been represented as genuine Darlings, a brief description of them might be useful. As mentioned above, the fastest way to tell them apart is that they are usually made of brass. True Darlings are iron and steel. The Swedish pistols, while existing in various forms, just about all have a very distinctive rounded collar at the breech, which can be seen clearly in the photograph shown here. They tend to be signed by the maker "J. Engh" or with groups of three initials, such as IEH, AGS and AIS.[47]

Johan Engholm (1820–1918) was a gunsmith from Hestra, Odestugu in Sweden. He also made brass candlesticks and chandeliers.[48]

Given all of this confusing misinformation, it shouldn't surprise us that although the Darling was the first patented pepperbox in the United States and an important part of revolver development, the only accurate information known about this pistol for decades was what could be seen in the illustrations and description included with the April 13, 1836 patent. In this document, the Darling brothers described their invention, which they called a Rotary Pistol:

…the "rotary pistol"…consists of six bores or barrels united, cut out of a single piece of steel placed in a circle parallel with each and surrounding a common center or bore, which center bore is for the reception of an iron axle around which the barrels are to revolve. One end of this axle is fastened into the stock of the piece at the breech of the barrels, and the end at the mouths of the barrels is fitted for the reception of a screw. This screw runs into the axle in a direction parallel to its axis, and the screw prevents the barrels from slipping off from the axle.

The lock of the pistol is in common form, containing a mainspring, a dog, and trigger for the moving of a common percussion hammer or cock.

There is placed on the axle, before mentioned, a revolving flat ring or washer, between the breech of the barrels and the stock. On the side of this ring toward the barrels is fixed a small cog or spring, which is fitted to play into notches cut into the breech, in a direction parallel with the axis of the axle, in the manner of a rag-wheel. [Note: A rag-wheel was a kind of gear, see footnote.[49]] *There are six of these notches in the breech, one for each barrel. To the side of this ring next to the stock is attached a small lever resting on a prop or fulcrum placed at a suitable distance from the breech. This lever is moved by a hand or stirrup fastened to the hammer, and instead of the flat ring or washer a spring-hook is attached to the end of the lever. By drawing back the hammer to a cock the lever is depressed, and the aforesaid ring, with its cog, is moved on the axle from the left to the right and carries forward the barrels, bringing the nipple of the barrel directly under the hammer. The motion of the hammer, in striking the nipple and cap, raises the lever, carries back the ring and cog far enough to catch into the next notch. By drawing back the hammer the first motion is repeated, and so on till each nipple of each barrel is successively brought under the hammer for discharge. Each barrel has its separate nipple at the breech, and the barrels of said pistol are charged for firing in the usual manner of other fire-arms.*

The Darling Pepperbox

UNITED STATES PATENT OFFICE.

BARTON DARLING AND BENJAMIN DARLING, OF BELLINGHAM, MASS.

IMPROVEMENT IN PISTOLS AND SHORT FIRE-ARMS.

Specification forming part of Letters Patent No.███, dated April 13, 1836.

To all whom it may concern:

Be it known that we, BARTON DARLING and BENJAMIN DARLING, both of Bellingham, in the county of Norfolk and State of Massachusetts, have invented a new and useful Improvement in the Construction of Pistols and Short Fire-Arms; and I do hereby declare that the following is a full and exact description of said improvement, and of the construction and operation of the said pistol and fire-arms, as invented and improved by us, viz: We call the same the "rotary pistol;" and it consists of six bores or barrels united, cut out of a single piece of steel placed in a circle parallel with each and surrounding a common center or bore, which center bore is for the reception of an iron axle around which the barrels are to revolve. One end of this axle is fastened into the stock of the piece at the breech of the barrels, and the end at the mouths of the barrels is fitted for the reception of a screw. This screw runs into the axle in a direction parallel to its axis, and the screw prevents the barrels from slipping off from the axle.

The lock of the pistol is in common form, containing a mainspring, a dog, and trigger for the moving of a common percussion hammer or cock.

There is placed on the axle, before mentioned, a revolving flat ring or washer, between the breech of the barrels and the stock. On the side of this ring toward the barrels is fixed a small cog or spring, which is fitted to play into notches cut into the breech, in a direction parallel with the axis of the axle, in the manner of a rag-wheel. There are six of these notches in the breech, one for each barrel. To the side of this ring next to the stock is attached a small lever resting on a prop or fulcrum placed at a suitable distance from the breech. This lever is moved by a hand or stirrup fastened to the hammer, and instead of the flat ring or washer a spring-hook is attached to the end of the lever. By drawing back the hammer to a cock the lever is depressed, and the aforesaid ring, with its cog, is moved on the axle from left to right and carries forward the barrels, bringing the nipple of the barrel directly under the hammer. The motion of the hammer, in striking the nipple and cap, raises the lever, carries back the ring and cog far enough to catch into the next notch. By drawing back the hammer the first motion is repeated, and so on till each nipple of each barrel is successively brought under the hammer for discharge. Each barrel has its separate nipple at the breech, and the barrels of said pistol are charged for firing in the usual manner of other fire-arms.

The machine work of the pistol and lock is concealed within the stock, except the hammer above and the trigger and guard below the same. The stock of the pistol may be made of malleable cast-iron, common wrought-iron, or other malleable metal.

What we claim as our own invention, and not previously known in the above-described pistol, is—

The six or more bores in a single piece of steel, as described above, also the rotary motion as mentioned in the specification and applied to the bores of the said pistol, and also the making of the stock of said pistol of malleable cast-iron or wrought-iron or other malleable metal.

BARTON DARLING.
BENJAMIN M. DARLING.

Witnesses:
WILLARD THAYER,
JOHN WANELL.

The machine work of the pistol and lock is concealed within the stock, except the hammer above and the trigger and guard below the same. The stock of the pistol may be made of malleable cast-iron, common wrought-iron, or other malleable metal.

The features specifically listed by the Darling brothers as innovations "not previously known" are the six or more bores in a single piece

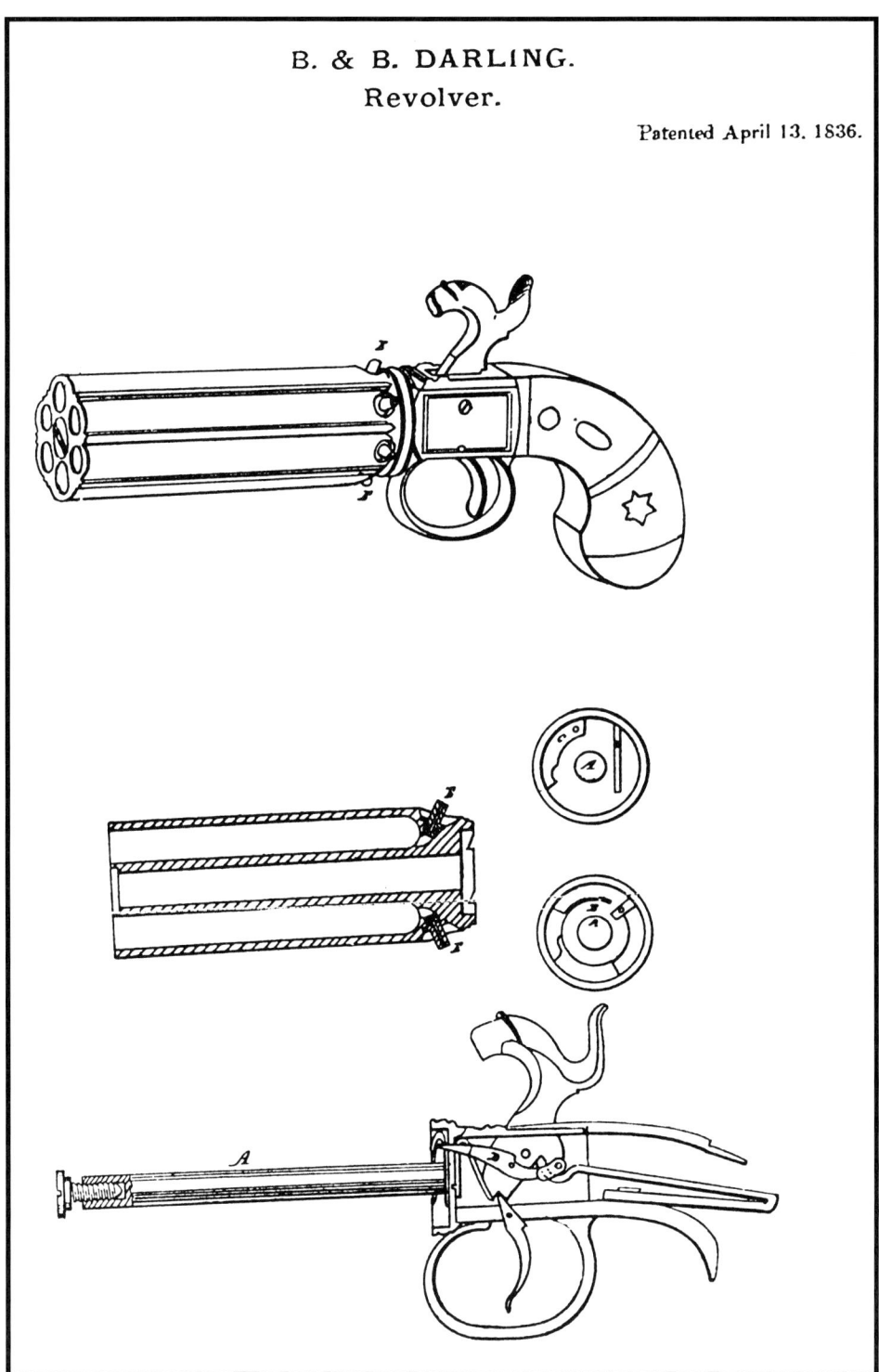

of steel, the rotary motion and the malleable metal stock.

One thing that is quite interesting about the pepperbox patent is that the invention looks, structurally, a lot like the earlier Darling patent for water wheels. In particular, the notched plate that makes up the rotating mechanism of the revolving pepperbox looks very similar to the plate on their water wheel, which was made out of iron. Both inventions were patented in the same year by members of the same family and I find it hard to believe that this is a coincidence.

The rotation mechanism is the most important aspect of the pepperbox patent and the part of the pistol that is the most confusing to understand. For this reason, a detailed explanation of the mechanism is provided on the following two pages. Many photographs and drawings have been included, and it is hoped that the reader will be able to learn how the rotation of the pistol operated.

The pistol that the Darling brothers patented and manufactured survives today in very limited numbers. In fact, it is quite possible for an American pepperbox collector to go his whole life without seeing one in person. The example owned by author Lou Winant, serial number 113, was one of the earliest known to experts. Winant thought it so very valuable that he kept it in a safe-deposit box at his bank. When he finally decided to sell his Darling he offered it in a strange "reverse auction." He notified all interested parties that the price would start at $3,000 and go down $100 per day starting on June 1, 1955. The first "bidder" who called him would be the winner. His fellow collectors did not appreciate this scheme and no one decided to bid. Eventually, he sold the pistol to his friend Frank Horner.

The differences between surviving specimens of the Darling pepperbox are purely cosmetic; they have a "cookie cutter" similarity that we usually associate with later periods of gunmaking. When I talk about this similarity, I mean that they have an unusual amount of uniformity as compared to other firearms and products of their day. This should not be confused with the kind of identical uniformity seen today, in Coke bottles for instance. During the early 19th century, there was still a "craftsman" rather than a "factory" mentality at work in the guns made in America — especially those made for the civilian, rather than military trade. There is quite a bit of variety amongst surviving Darling pistols when it comes to their decoration and grip materials, but the profile, size, mechanical design and construction of parts is more-or-less identical. The Darlings bridge the gap between the gunsmiths of a previous

The Darling Pepperbox

The cylinders from two different Darling pepperboxes. Even though the condition of the cylinders is very different, it is still easy to see just how identical they are. One of the distinguishing features of Darling pepperboxes is just how "cookie cutter" identical some of their major parts are.

generation, who had made each gun a little differently, and the gunmakers of the following generation, whose factories cranked out thousands of guns according to designated "models," each matching the other in almost all particulars.

Physically, Darling pepperboxes have an overall size of almost exactly 7". The barrel cluster measures precisely 3.25" from the muzzle to the breech and is 1-3/8" in diameter. There are six barrels, each having a caliber of .30.

The thing that I notice most when I have a number of Darling pepperboxes on hand for comparison is how amazingly identical the cylinders are. Machined from a single

The Darling Pepperbox

The Rotation Mechanism Exposed!

The rotation mechanism of the Darling pepperbox is difficult to understand even when you have one in your own hand. However, with the aid of photographs and drawings, perhaps the motions of the various parts can be made clear.

When the screw is removed from the muzzle end of the barrel cluster, the barrel cluster can then slide off along a metal rod. Here you can see the pistol's body with the barrel cluster removed and the screw back in place at the end of the rod.

The mechanism is now exposed at the base of the rod.
On top of the mechanism is a large washer with portions of it cut out, including a deep notch. A bent-up spring is pinned to the top. This washer is a free moving piece that can be slid down the rod and taken off. With the washer removed, the breech face is revealed. On the right, there is a slot cut out of the breech face and the tip of a rotation lever or "hand" can be seen extending from the pistol's interior. The other feature on the breech face is a small spring with one end attached by a pin to the breech, similar to the spring on the washer; the free, lower end is bent up in the air.

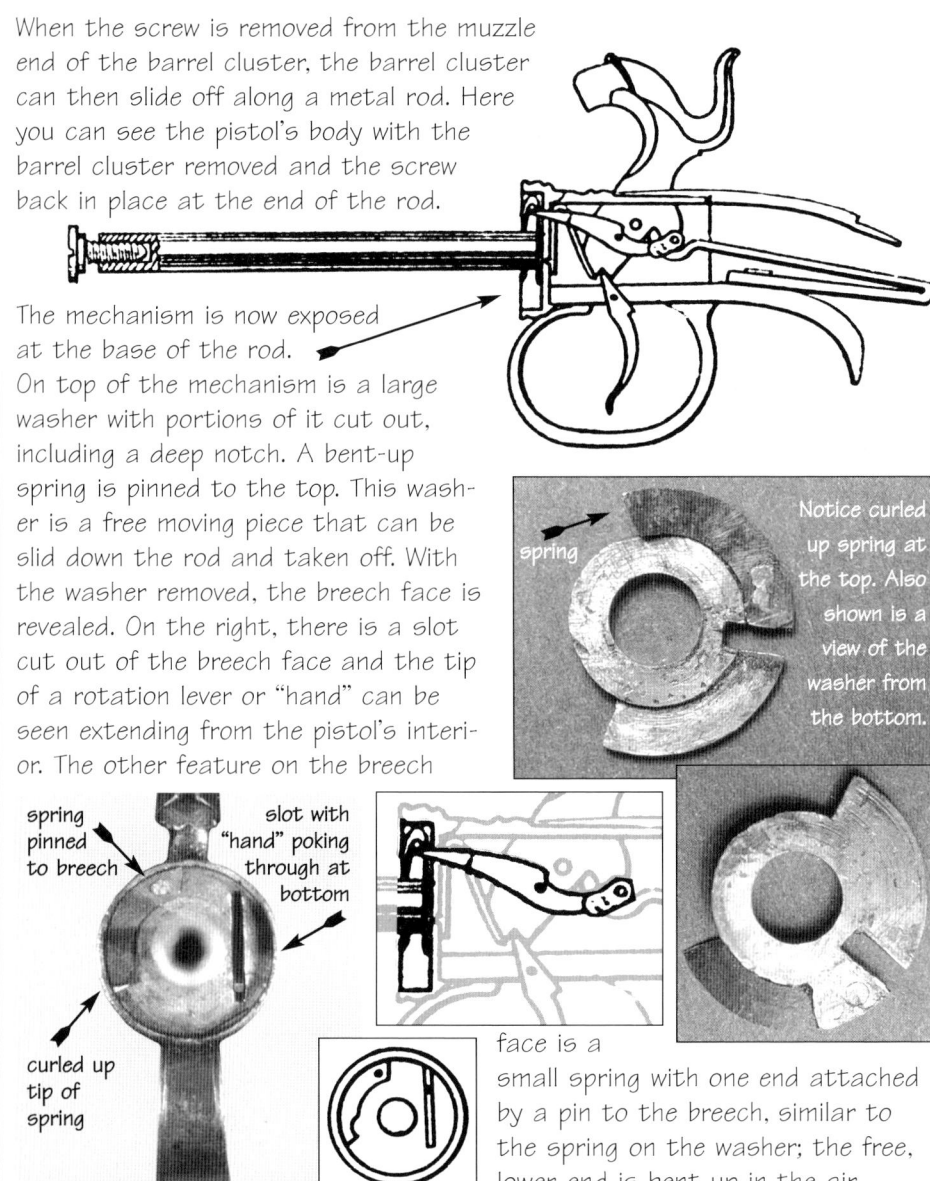

Notice curled up spring at the top. Also shown is a view of the washer from the bottom.

spring pinned to breech

slot with "hand" poking through at bottom

curled up tip of spring

— 64 —

We have shown and described all of the parts of the rotation mechanism. Now we will see how they work.

The washer is slid back in place so that it sits on the breech face. The little notch on the right side of the washer has the rotation hand sticking through it and the large section missing from the washer on the left side entirely exposes the spring that is pinned to the breech face.

Now the barrel cluster is slid back down the rod and screwed into place. Notice that there are notches in the breech end of the barrel cluster. One

breech face spring exposed through gap in washer

washer is slid down rod, back in place on top of breech face

rotation hand sticking through little notch in washer

MECHANISM IN ITS UNCOCKED POSITION

of these notches will catch on the tip of the bent up spring on the washer. There are six of these notches, one for each shot that the pistol can take. When the pistol is cocked, the hand will move up the slot in the breech face, pushing the washer around about 60 degrees counterclockwise. The curled up spring end at the top of the washer will in turn push the barrel cluster around so that the next barrel is ready to fire, with the percussion nipple in position under the hammer. Upon firing, the rotation hand drops to its original position at the bottom of the slot in the breech face. This motion pushes the washer back to where it started, with the tip of the washer's spring engaging in a new notch in the barrel cluster. The small spring pinned to the breech face stops the washer from over rotating. The pistol is now ready to be cocked and fired again.

washer spring tip has pushed cylinder around as part of the cocking motion

rotation hand has slid up slot in breech face, pushing the washer around

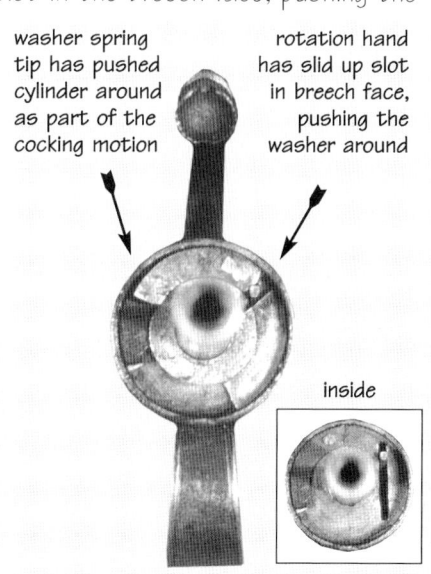

inside

MECHANISM IN ITS COCKED POSITION

Another photograph of two Darling cylinders, again showing just how similar these pieces are to each other and how much regularity there was in the manufacturing process. This view, from the muzzle end, shows the six barrels. The center hole is where the axle rod goes, and this end of it is capped by a slotted screw.

piece of solid steel, it really isn't fair to call them barrel clusters. You can actually line two pistols up, muzzle to muzzle, and the two will make an almost seamless whole. It is difficult to notice any differences, pistol to pistol. Templates must have been used to achieve this kind of uniformity, which was a very advanced technique for the 1830s. Also, it is my firm feeling that the barrel units were machined many at a time from a long section of steel, and then cut into their final lengths after the fluting and shaping had been done for the whole length.

Originally, I had assumed that the hammers on these pepperboxes were parts that had been purchased by the Darlings from an outside source. It was common for New England

The Darling Pepperbox

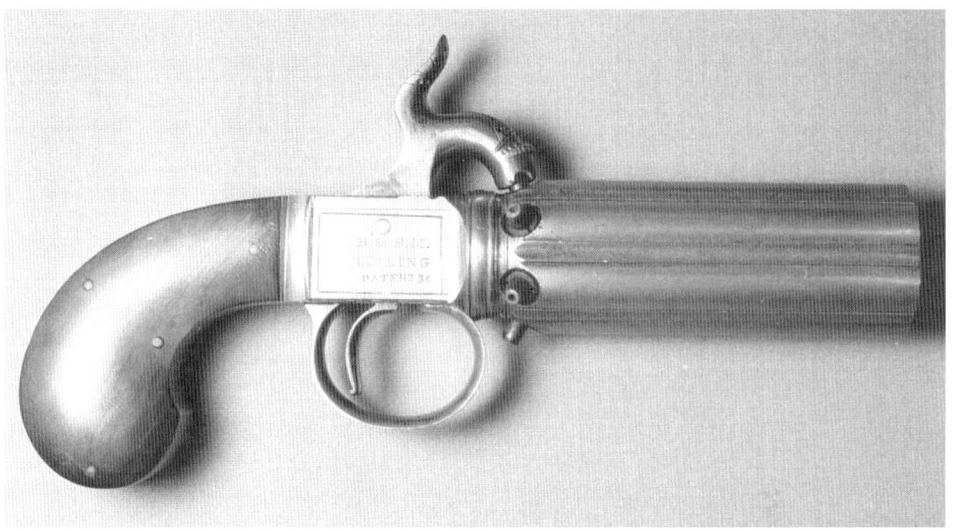

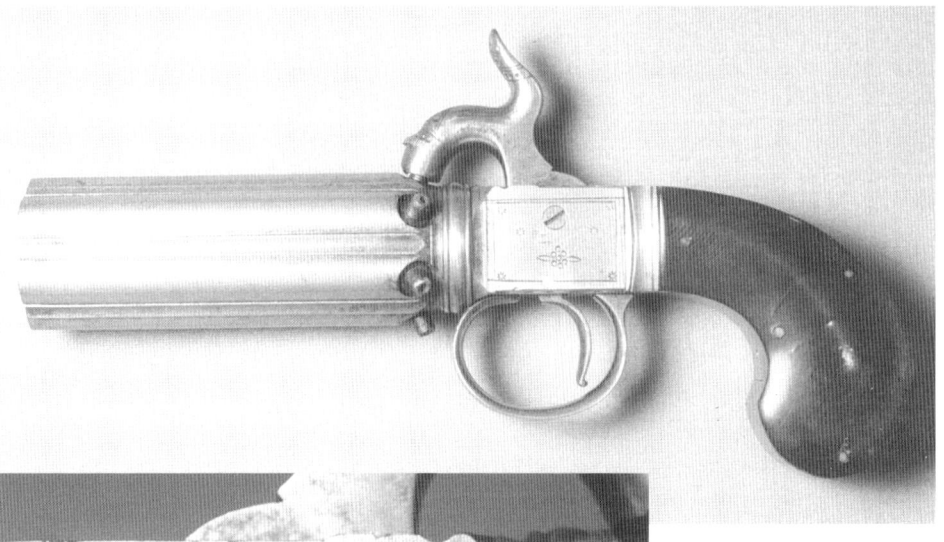

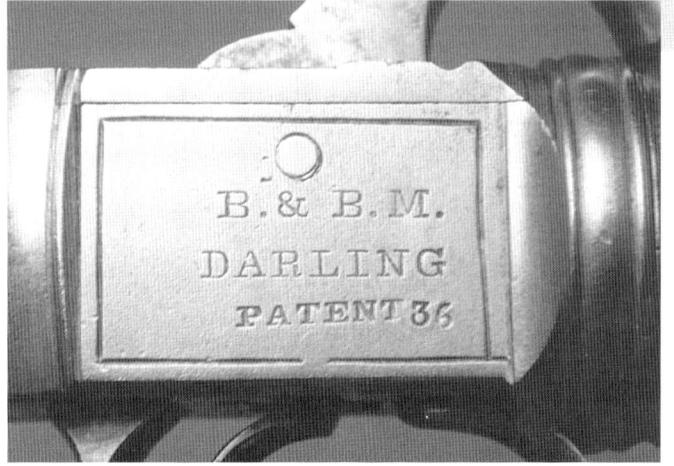

Darling pepperbox serial number 36. This is a very attractive pistol, with a particularly fancy decoration on the hammer. (Photography of this pistol was allowed through the kindness of Richard Littlefield.)

The Darling Pepperbox

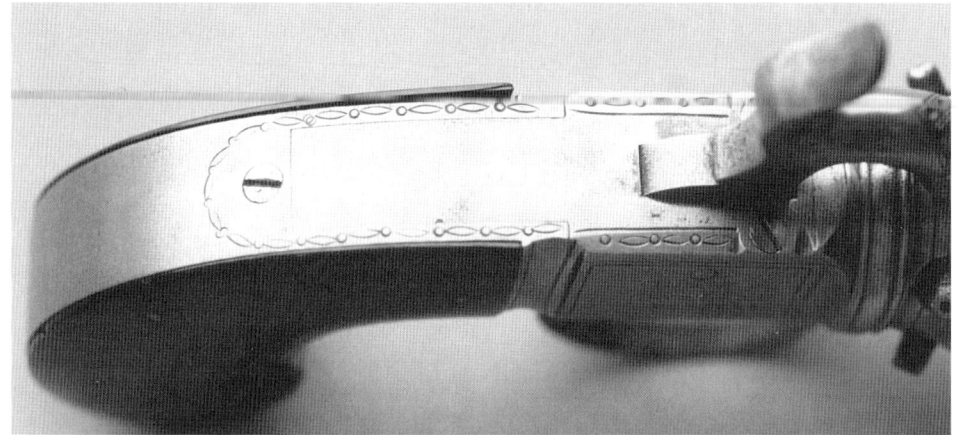

Close-up views of the decoration on pistol number 36. The top strap design is found on many Darlings and is very typical. The hammer decoration is a particularly ornate form of a design favored by the Darlings and seen on some of their other nice pepperboxes, like number 115.

(Photography of this pistol was allowed through the kindness of Richard Littlefield.)

The Darling Pepperbox

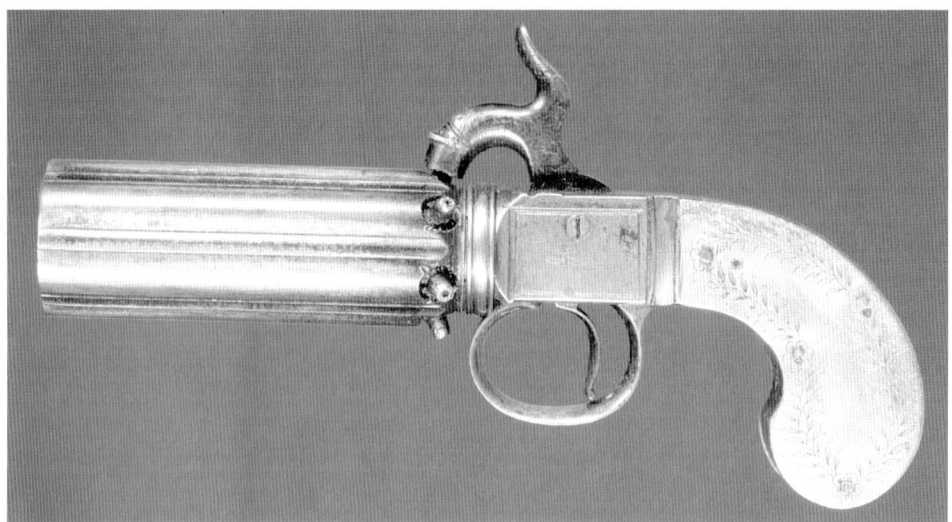

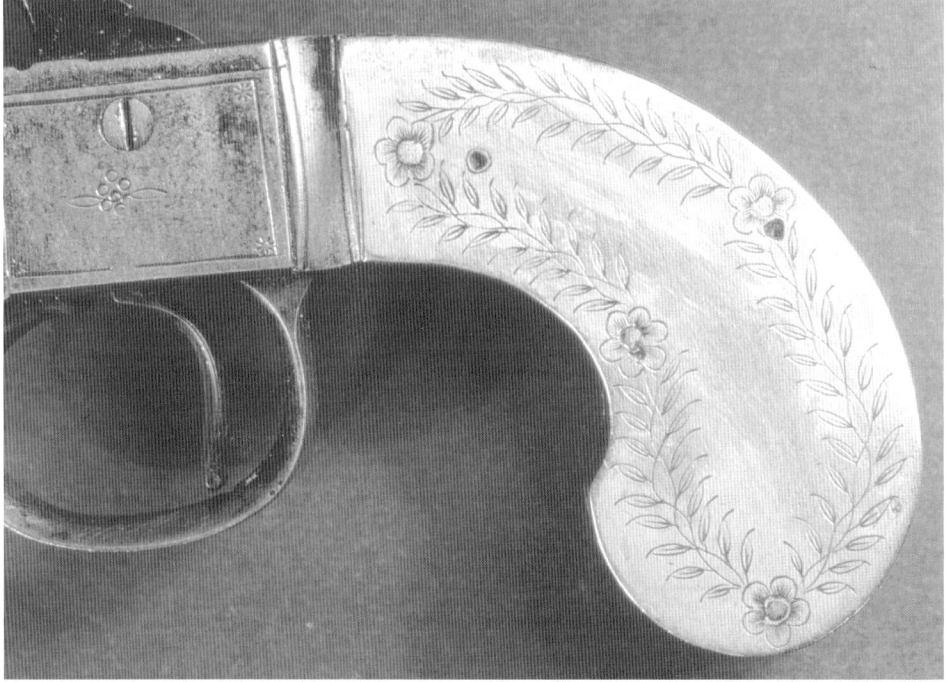

Darling pepperbox, serial number 54. This is the only Darling so far observed with these distinctive german or nickel silver grips. (Howard Miller collection)

gunsmiths of this era to buy many of the more complex or intricately-shaped gun parts "ready made" from a hardware store or specialist manufacturer. However, the hammers found on surviving Darling pistols are similar enough to each other so as to indicate common construc-

The Darling Pepperbox

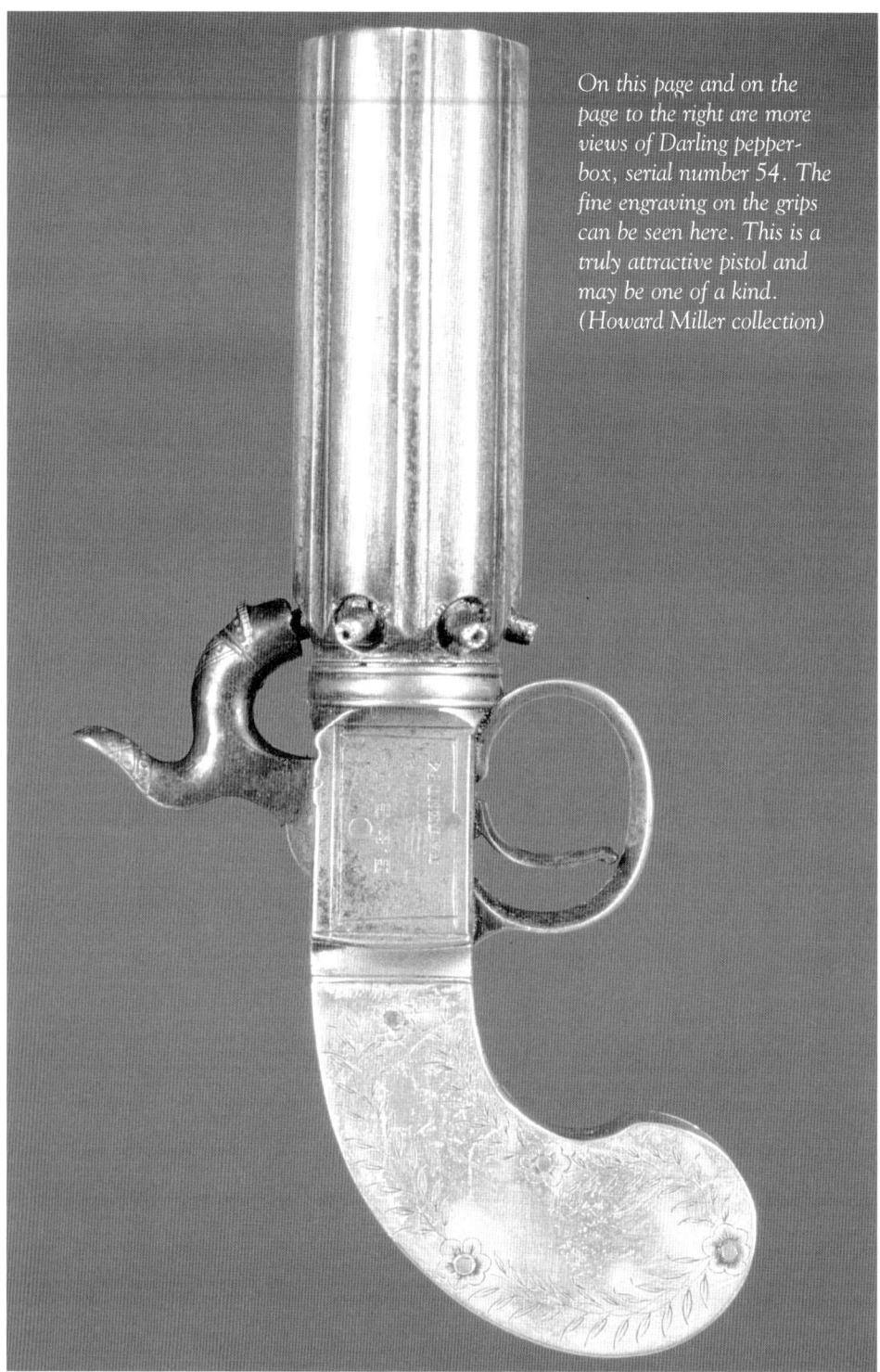

On this page and on the page to the right are more views of Darling pepperbox, serial number 54. The fine engraving on the grips can be seen here. This is a truly attractive pistol and may be one of a kind. (Howard Miller collection)

The Darling Pepperbox

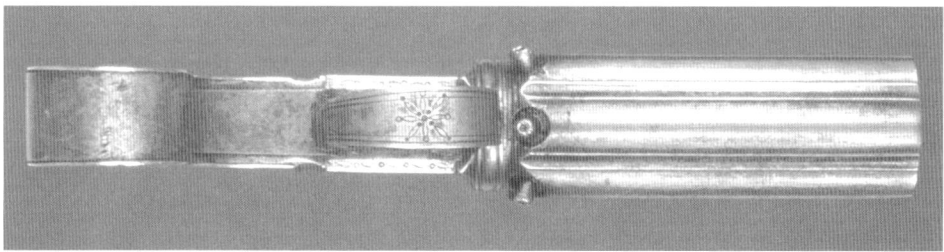

tion. Unless the Darlings just bought one huge batch when they started making pistols, we should probably assume that the hammers were made from scratch by the brothers themselves. The lavish decoration and extensive shaping seen on some of these hammers would seem to support this theory, as well.

The decoration on these pistols is usually frugal yet stylish. In the most common version, tortoise shell or dark wood grips are set off by german silver inlays that can come in the shape of diamonds, stars, circles, bands or simple pins. These guns are barrel heavy, which gives them a poor sense of proportion, but it would be a mistake to say that they are not very attractive. Engraving all appears to have been done by a common hand, with classic, simple motifs predominating.

The pistols are generally stamped "B. & B.M./DARLING/PATENT [serial number]" on one side and "WARRANTED" on the

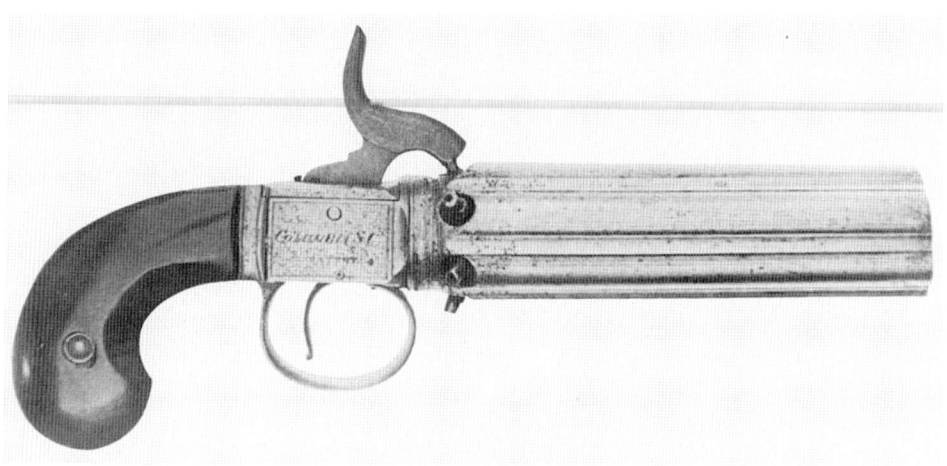

The Darling pepperbox marked "W. GLAZE" on the left side and "COLUMBIA, S.C." over "PATENT 4" on the right side. Because this pistol was once owned by Sam Smith, who wrote an article about it, this has become a very well known gun. Its southern association gives it added interest. Aside from this gun's unusually long cylinder, other parts that do not seem to look like typical Darling construction are the hammer and the grips. (Photo taken while this pistol was in the Sam Smith collection.)

other. Often, "WARRANTED" is replaced with a simple design. There are variations on this theme, and indeed, some have no markings or serial numbers at all. Also, as was discussed earlier, some of the pistols have different names on them altogether. The Darlings did not have the kind of retail establishment that would have allowed them to sell scores of pistols, so they depended upon wholesalers and dealers to introduce their pepperboxes to the public. At least one known Darling bears the name of a dealer and there may be more because this was a normal business practice during those days.

The pistol with a known dealer name on it has been discussed and illustrated in a number of articles and books, and has become quite a famous gun. Once in the Sam Smith collection, it bears the markings "W. GLAZE" and "COLUMBIA, S.C./PATENT 4". It is assumed that the number four is a serial number and may be part of the normal serial number range. Aside from its lack of the normal markings, it is a standard Darling in shape and operation except that its barrel cluster is longer than expected. The cylinder or barrel cluster's total

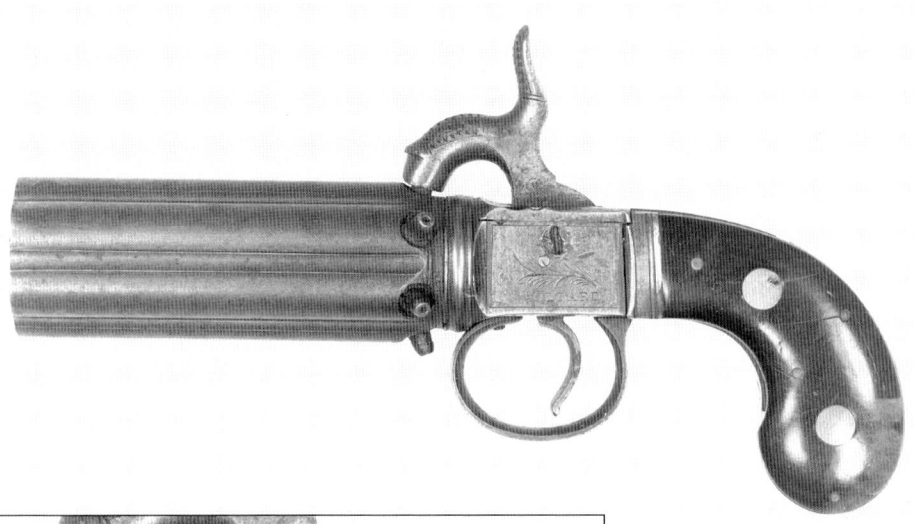

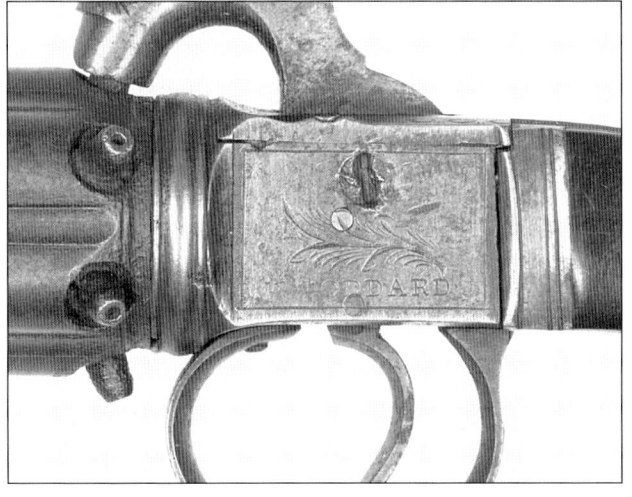

Darling pepperbox marked "Goddard". While this pistol has been explained as a dealer-marked example, it could also be the name of the owner that we are seeing here on the pistol's frame. Some have read this marking as "STODDARD". The marking is too faint on the left to tell for sure. (Photograph courtesy of the Olin Corporation)

length is an inch more than normal, giving the pistol an overall length of eight inches instead of the expected seven. As has been discussed elsewhere, the cylinders on Darlings are remarkably consistent in all respects, so this one inch difference is a significant deviation from the norm. Also, the "Glaze" pistol has a different style of hammer than is found on other known Darlings; this again is a feature that is unexpected. Lastly, the grips have a somewhat different construction than other observed specimens. While a number of explanations have been suggested concerning this pepperbox, with no clear answers available, it remains a unique and intriguing pistol.[50]

Another example often described as a distributor-marked Darling is the one marked "Goddard". Because it was a part of

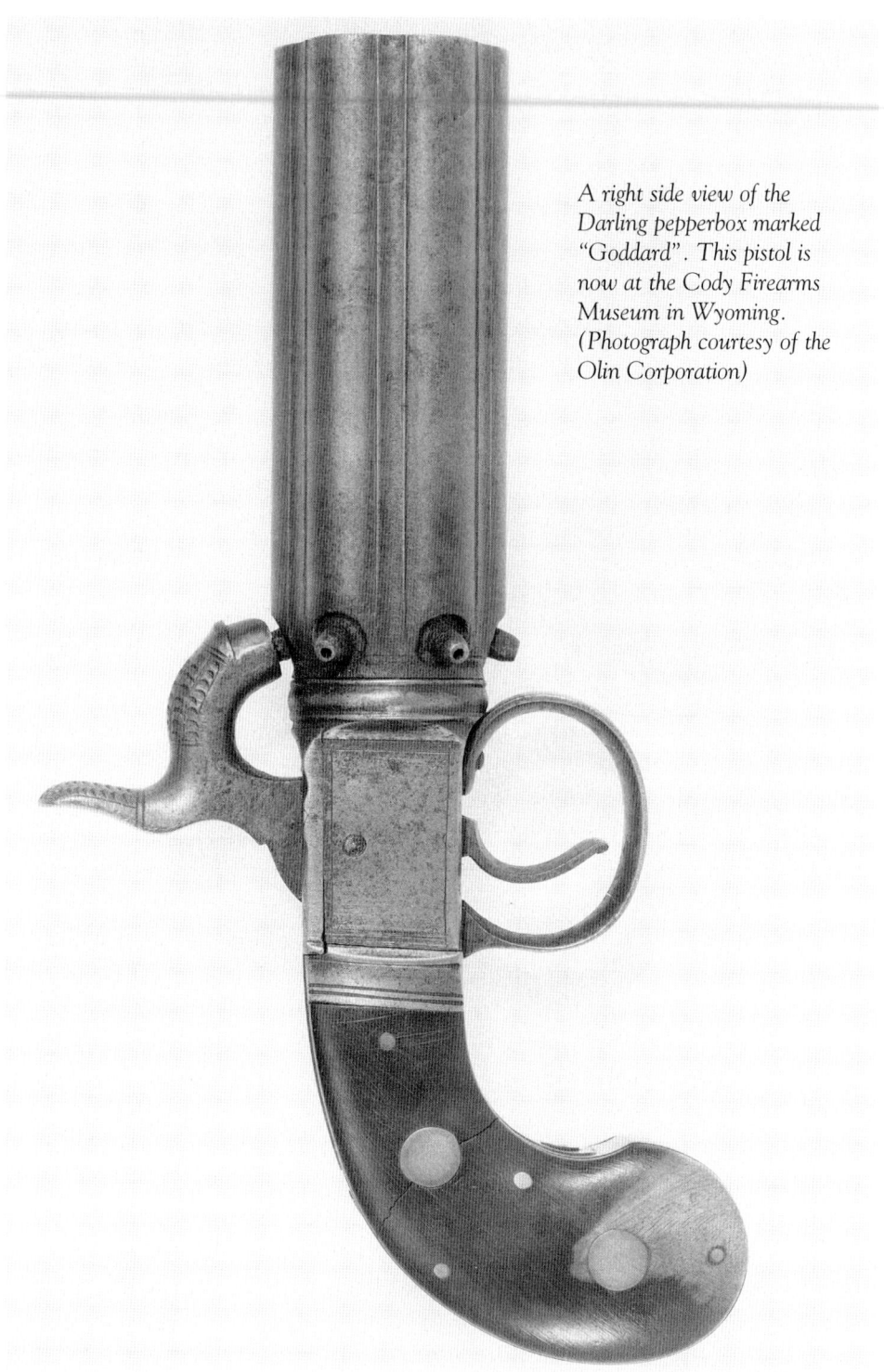

A right side view of the Darling pepperbox marked "Goddard". This pistol is now at the Cody Firearms Museum in Wyoming. (Photograph courtesy of the Olin Corporation)

The Goddard-marked pistol was originally in the personal collection of famous gun designer and Winchester executive Edwin Pugsley. To the right is his handwritten file card for the pistol. Note that Pugsley says the pistol rotates by hand. While I have not been able to disassemble this gun to check, I can only presume that it is a revolving gun with a broken mechanism. Edwin Pugsley was the inspiration for the Charles Addams "Addams Family" cartoon character "Pugsley". Winchester later purchased most of Pugsley's guns for their corporate collection.

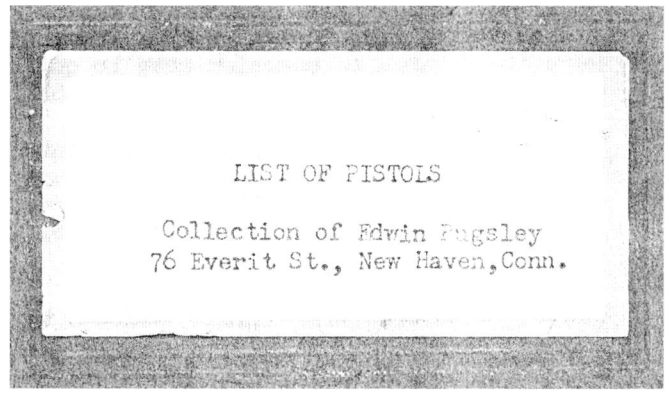

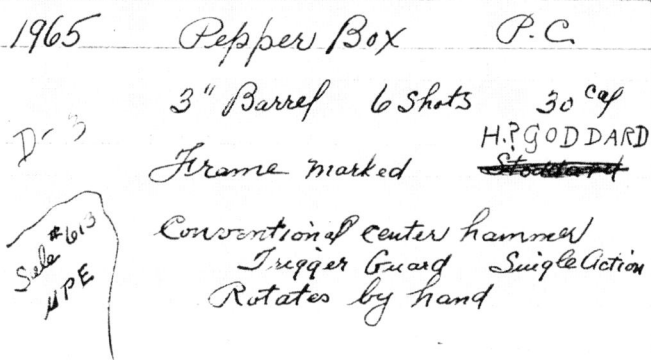

Winchester's well-known factory collection, it has often been discussed in books. Unnumbered, this pepperbox's decoration is limited to two circular inlays with one pin at the top, and is fairly austere by Darling standards. While it is possible that Goddard was a dealer, there are no obvious candidates of which I am aware. Perhaps the name on this pistol is its owner's rather than that of its seller. The Goddards were, and still are, a prominent family in Rhode Island society and this possibility should not be discounted.

Yet another Darling with a different marking on it is the one sold by the Greg Martin auction house in February of 2003. This pistol is interesting in that it bears no markings except a stamped "D" within a circle on the lower tang. I have handled this pistol at length and am convinced that both the pistol and the mark are genuine. It seems obvious that the mark is a maker's mark for the Darlings, although I am aware of no other guns bearing this mark. One theory that has been put forth in this book is that the Darlings probably made other guns besides their pepperboxes. Perhaps we will some day find an otherwise unsigned

The Darling Pepperbox

Darling pepperbox with no markings except for the hitherto unknown D in a circle, which is thought to be a Darling maker's mark. Another view of this gun is shown on the facing page. (Thanks are extended to Greg Martin for allowing photography of this pistol.)

firearm that bears this Darling mark, and therefore learn more about their other gunmaking activities.

Because of the use of iron as a construction material on these pistols, some of them survive in poor shape today, scarred by corrosion. The grips, if made of tortoise shell, are prone to cracking, and a couple of the wood-gripped examples seem as if they could be

The Darling Pepperbox

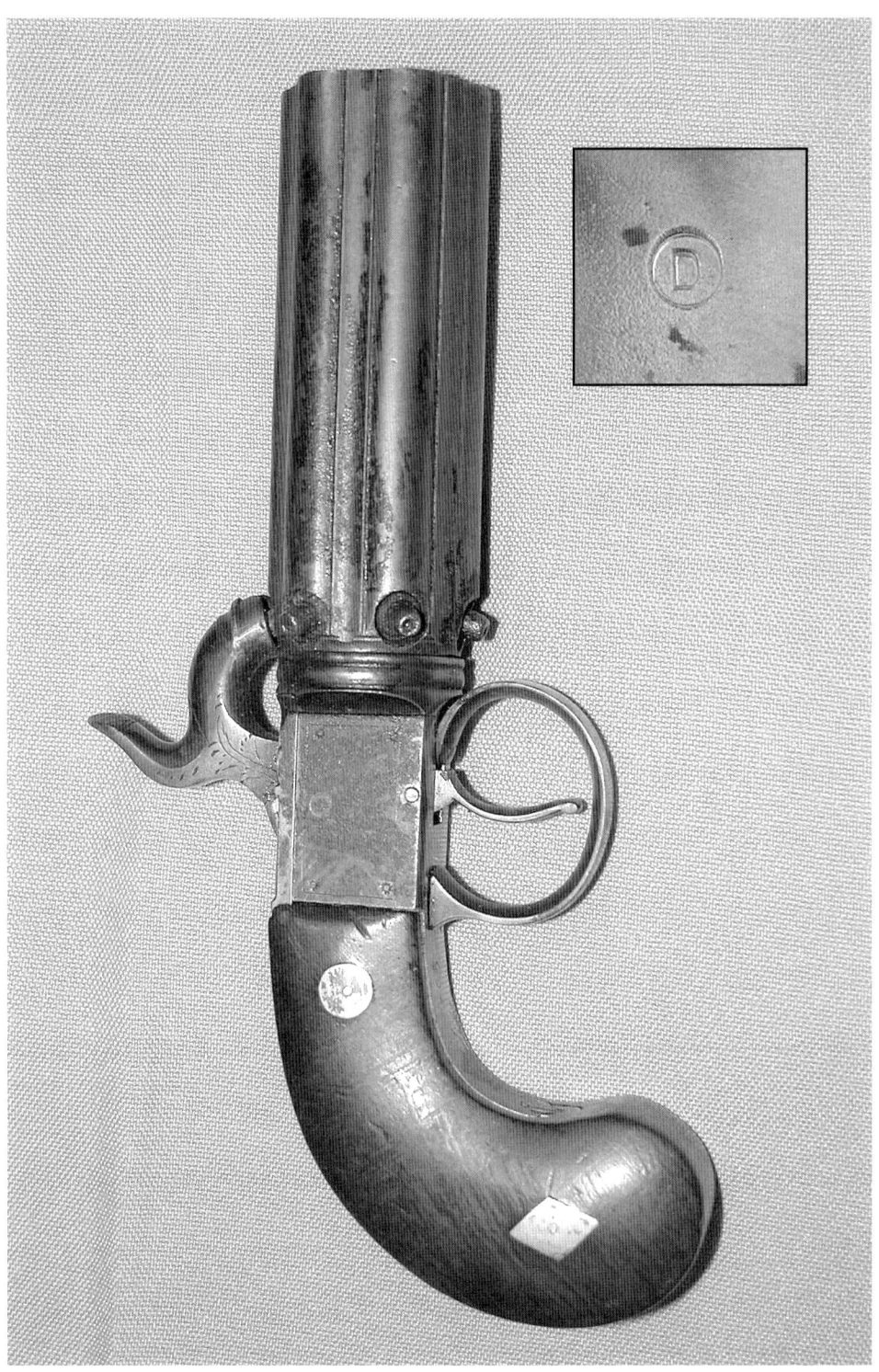

The Darling Pepperbox

A Darling pepperbox in original condition, but showing a great deal of corrosion. Despite the pitting on the frame, it can be seen that this Darling is marked conventionally and the serial number is thought to be a "10". Other views of this gun are shown on the facing page.

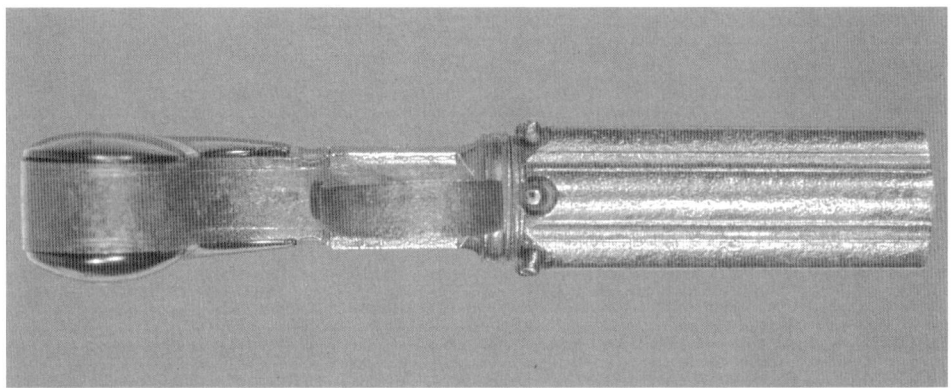

replacements for the tortoise grips that have broken and become lost. Also, the rotating mechanism is broken on many of the pistols encountered. The parts of the mechanism most likely to break are the tip of the "hand" that extends from the lock, and the tips of the two springs shown in the "mechanism exposed" description earlier. For these reasons, a Darling pepperbox in top condition is quite a rarity and should not be purchased without a considerable amount of careful inspection. However, some excellent examples do survive and those lucky enough to own one have a treasure to be cherished.

    While there is room for argument concerning exactly when the Darlings stopped production, it doesn't take much imagination to understand why it happened. As can be seen from the limited number of surviving pistols, this product just never "took off." The fatal blow for the Darling was almost certainly the growing popularity of the superior Allen Pepperbox, which fired more quickly with a compact, double-action mechanism. Ethan Allen, also a Bellingham, Massachusetts native, simply had a better product and one that would sell in countless numbers over the following decades.

It must have frustrated the Darling brothers that Allen made such a success in the pepperbox business when he was almost certainly inspired in that direction by the Darlings themselves. Ethan Allen, born in 1806, was eight years younger than Barton Darling, and as was discussed earlier, almost certainly spent considerable time at the Darling shop, maybe even working there. And while the Allen pepperbox had the advantage of a rapid fire, double action mechanism, the Darling pepperbox was perhaps a better made pistol and should have benefited from its earlier date of introduction.

But unfortunately for the Darlings, Allen had some advantages that they did not. First of all, in partnership with his university-educated

---

So often, when we are studying early factories, it is difficult to discover what it was actually like to work in the shop itself. Below is an extract from *Confessions of Boyhood* by John Albee, a Bellingham youngster who served as an apprentice in the Allen & Thurber factory:

Two of my sister's influential patrons [had a business that] was the manufacture of pistols, a patented, six-barrelled, self-cocking revolver, the first of its kind, I believe, ever invented, and a wonder of its day. The whole six barrels revolved on a rod running through their center, and by one and the same ratchet movement the hammer was raised and the chambers of the barrel thrown into position to receive the discharge from a percussion cap. There was a great demand for these pistols in the South and West. It was, I suppose, on account of my sister's intimacy with the families of these manufacturers that a place was found for me in their works.

See me no longer in a linen shirt and brown broadcloth jacket [the author's previous job had been in a store], but again in blue jean overalls, with grimy, oily hands and dirty face, shut in walls from which [there] was no escape for ten hours each day. The lathes, hand tools, forges and engine which operated the machinery were novel and interesting to me at first. I was the only boy in the establishment. The workmen, all skilled mechanics, were a remarkably fine body of men. They earned large wages, lived quite comfortably, and were prominent in their several circles and churches. One of them became Lieut. Gov. of Mass. I was placed under the charge of the foreman of the first floor where the heavier part of the material of the pistol was prepared. I did the odd jobs of the room, worked a punching machine and managed the lathe that turned the rough outside of the pistol barrel. My master took an active personal interest in me and was very minute and painstaking in his instructions. He was a very pious man and lost no opportunity of exhorting me to seek religion and become converted. It made no impression on me; I understood no word he said. Besides, just the same words had always been familiar to me and had never conveyed any meaning to my simple ears. It did not trouble me to be called a sinner; it never occurred to me to question whether I was or not... But when my master invited me to go a-fishing on some half holiday, that was a very different sort of a text, which I well understood. Alas, when the fish did not bite, it gave an uncomfortable opportunity for a little exhortation. In addition to the work of the shop I spent much time in the office, where I was employed in putting the last touches to the pistols before being packed for delivery. I burnished the silver plates, set in the handles, cleaned and oiled the chambers, hammers and nipples, and polished the whole with fine chamois skin. Thus I had a hand in the beginning and completion of the construction of a pistol, and knew pretty well all of the intermediate operations. I also obtained an inkling of the way the business was conducted by hearing the conversation and discussions of the proprietors. I heard many secrets. Some of them confused my small glimmerings of moral sense. It seemed to me that I had known the same sort of obliquities among boys in the swapping of jackknives. I heard the bookkeeper say one day, "business is business; this is no Sunday school." I had bewildering thoughts. Was it possible these pistols were not what they seemed and would not kill a man? For I knew that they were sold mostly in the South for the fighting of duels. I longed to try one on a cat."

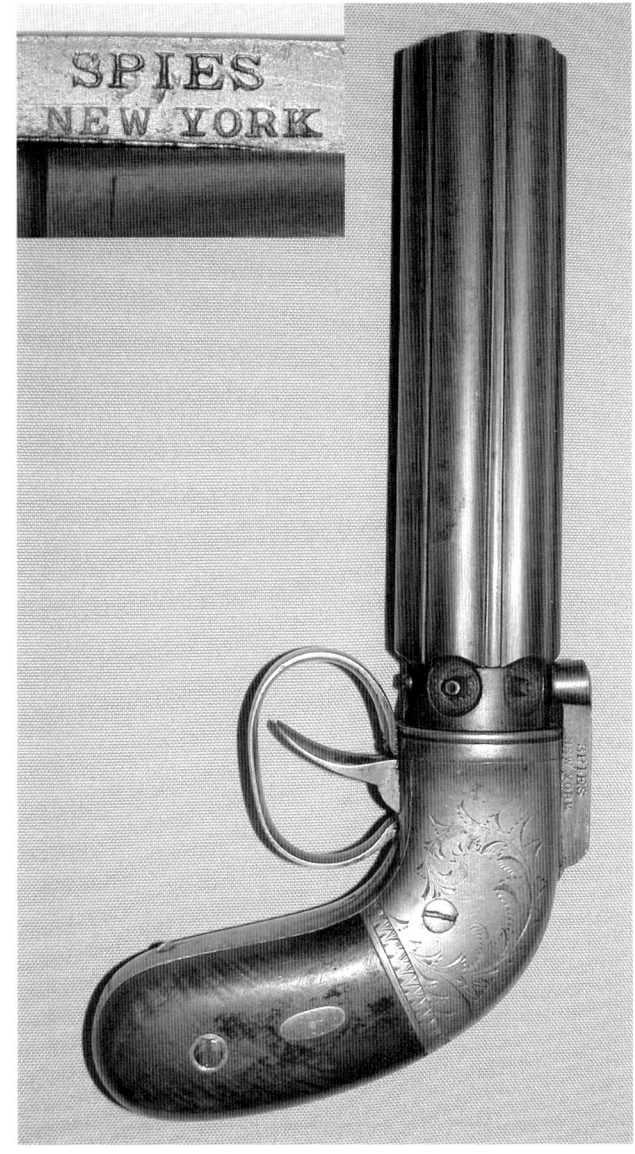

An early Allen & Thurber pepperbox pistol made in their Grafton, Massachusetts factory. These pistols were amazingly popular with immigrants heading West. The double action system used here was patented by Allen in 1837. Comparison of this Allen & Thurber pistol with a Darling shows many similarities, both in design and appearance. Perhaps most noticeable is the barrel cluster, which is made of the exact same kind of steel as a Darling, with drilling, turning and fluting that definitely give it a similar look. This particular Allen & Thurber was marketed by the New York City distributor A.W. Spies. Spies was an active promotor of the Allen design, claiming that he could sell as many pistols as they would be able to make. (Pistol courtesy of Robert Butterfield)

brother-in-law Charles Thurber, Allen was quickly able to expand his operation into a small factory with all the accompanying benefits of productivity and economy. Also, unlike the Darlings who had operated in a poor economic climate, Allen had the good luck of starting his business at the exact time when the United States was experiencing a huge wave of immigration and westward expansion. These factors would lead to enormous sales, making the Allen the most popular pistol in the country and quickly eclipsing its Darling predecessor.

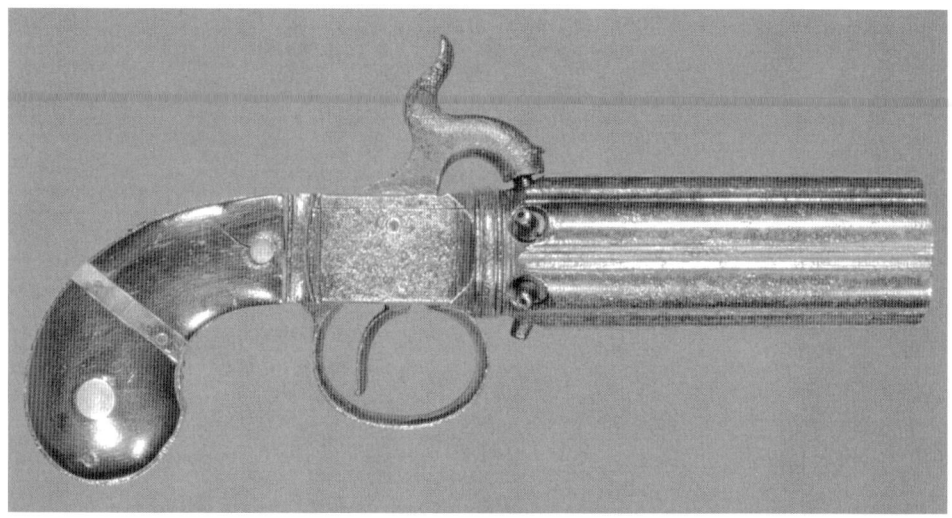

Two more views of the well worn Darling pepperbox thought to be serial number 10. The top view shows the overall pistol from the right. The grips are tortoise shell with nickel silver inlays. The bottom view shows the top of the grip strap. Notice the pleasing sunburst decoration around the screw.

When were Darling pepperboxes made?

To tell the truth, I'm kind of scared of this question because anything said here will probably be repeated over and over again as absolute fact, when the truth is far from certain.

Let's start with the beginning of production, because that's the easy part. Darlings were patented in 1836, displayed to the public in 1837, and advertised in 1838. Serial number 15 has the date "1836" on it in large lettering, but whether this indicates a year of production or the year of the patent is unknown. However, given the fact that the patent drawings depict a production Darling in all aspects, I think that it is fair to say that they were being made in

1836 and probably a bit earlier.

The question of when production stopped is more difficult. Their known advertising halted in 1839, the same year that the Bellingham pistol mill was sold and the brothers moved their residences to Woonsocket.[51] An argument could be made that this is when pistol production, or at least the bulk of it, was discontinued. The Darlings were doubtless engaged in numerous projects during their careers and just because they operated in Woonsocket is no proof that they actually made pistols there. However, I find three pieces of evidence fairly convincing. First, when Barton died he left a complete and organized set of tools and machines, with even some raw materials present. If you add this to the A.W. Spies ad reproduced earlier, and the fact that Alvin closed his Woonsocket mill upon Barton's death, you will have an inconclusive yet convincing case that pistols were made in Woonsocket.

Presuming, for the moment, that they did continue to make the occasional pistol in Woonsocket, we still have an absolute terminal date of 1848 when Barton died and the pistol making machinery was sold. Certainly, no pistols were made after that point.

Without further evidence to guide us, we would appear to have a main period of production from 1836 until 1839, with the near certainty of a few pistols having been made earlier than those dates and the strong likelihood that a group of pistols were made after those dates. Nothing, of course, seems to have been made after 1848.

How many Darling pepperboxes were made?

This is a difficult question to answer. Many New England pepperbox makers numbered their guns in series or batches. For instance, they would make one hundred guns and then start renumbering again at #1, repeating this process and thereby creating many guns with identical "serial" numbers. However, it is my personal belief that the numbers on Darlings are true serial numbers, and that each number is sequential and unique.

If this is true, then it should be simple to learn how many Darlings were made by finding the highest serial number. Unfortunately, the Darlings didn't make it so easy for us. First of all, some of the surviving pistols do not have serial numbers on them. Indeed, some of the examples that are illustrated and described in this book are not marked at all. Also, there is some question as to what we should regard as the highest observed serial number.

Serial Numbers Noted by the Author

#	Notes or Comments
4	Glaze example shown earlier.
5	Observed by Sam Smith.
10	Probably correct but hard to read. Shown in this book.
11	Mentioned and illustrated by Sam Smith in ASAC 1955 article and in Dunlap book. Very complicated grip decoration with three circles and one diagonal band. Two of the circles are surrounded by a pattern of pins, one pattern in a diamond shape and the other in a circle. This is the most elaborate grip treatment encountered thus far.
15	Marked "1836" on left side of frame, "B. & B.M. Darling, Patent 15" on right side of frame, tortoise shell grips, no inlays except four german silver pins. Shown in Dunlap book. The only known dated example.
36	Shown in this book.
54	Shown in this book.
95	Marty Glockner collection in Bellingham.
113	Lewis Winant kept this pistol in a safe deposit box, and tried to sell it by reverse auction. It was later purchased by pepperbox enthusiast Frank Horner and is now in the Frank Sellers collection. The pistol is illustrated twice in this book.
115	Shown in this book.
211	Shown in this book.

As can be seen in the table at left, the serial numbers end at 115 and then jump to 211. This is perplexing. As is described in the caption where pepperbox 211 is illustrated, there is some room for disagreement about what this number is meant to be, but I am very confident that it is a 211.

So perhaps our answer for how many Darlings were made should be slightly over two hundred pistols. However, I think that the truth is more complicated than that. Anyone studying the few Darling serial numbers available to us will notice that the numbers are not spread quite evenly across the sequence. This suggests that something else may be at work here. Author Jack Dunlap wrote that there could be gaps in the numbers represented by other guns that were not pepperboxes. This certainly seems possible, because the

The Darling Pepperbox

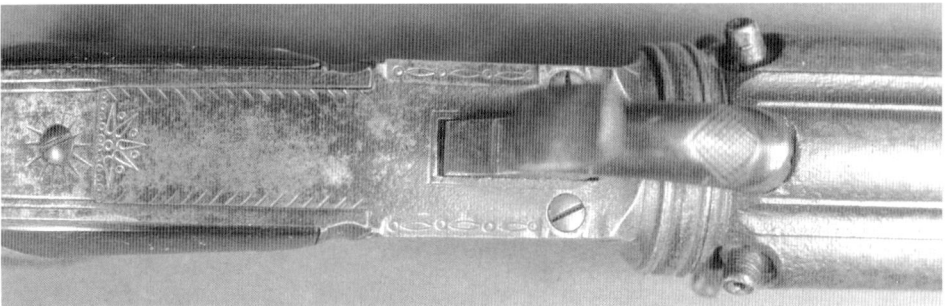

Darling pepperbox thought to be serial number 211. The owner of this pistol, however, reads the number as either a 277 or a 2TT. While the last two digits do have strong serifs, they match the "1"s on other Darlings. The silver band crossing the grip bears the initials "W.A.F.", those of the owner. This is a real sweetheart of a pistol and is one of my very favorites. (Howard Miller collection)

Darlings were from a gunsmithing family and probably produced other types of guns, perhaps without marking them with the Darling name because they were not their own patented products.

Another idea worth exploring is that the brothers rounded up to a higher number (200, for example) when resuming operations at a new location such as Woonsocket. Businesses today often do this with the numbers on their bank checks, starting a new sequence with a high number (1,000 for instance) which has nothing to do with the number of checks

The Darling Pepperbox

Darling pepperbox serial number 211. Notice the faint "WARRANTED" stamping in the bottom photo. Warranted was an assurance of quality often seen on Birmingham, England-made locks popular in New England. (Howard Miller collection)

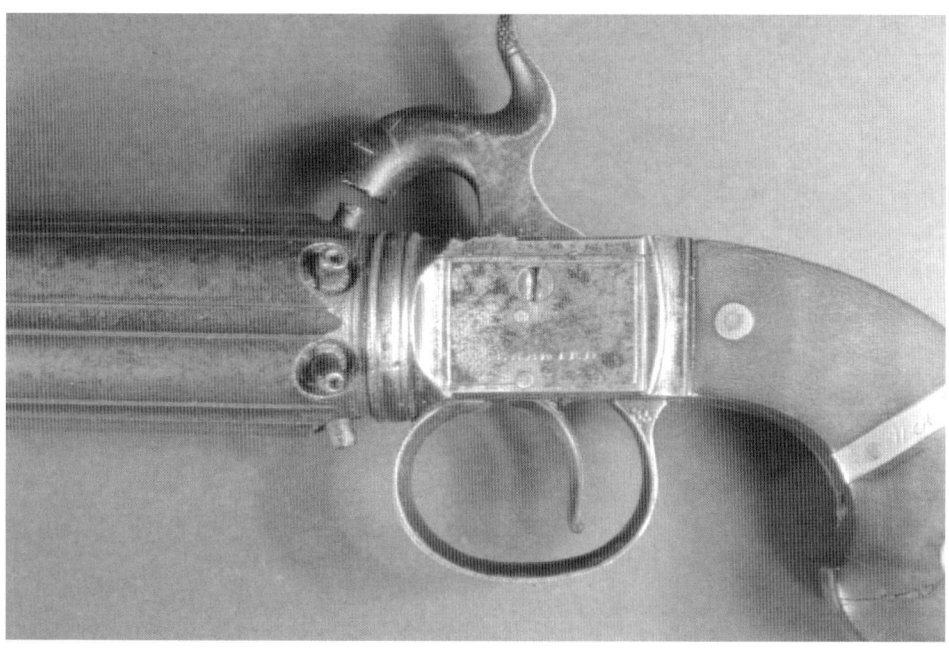

The Darling Pepperbox

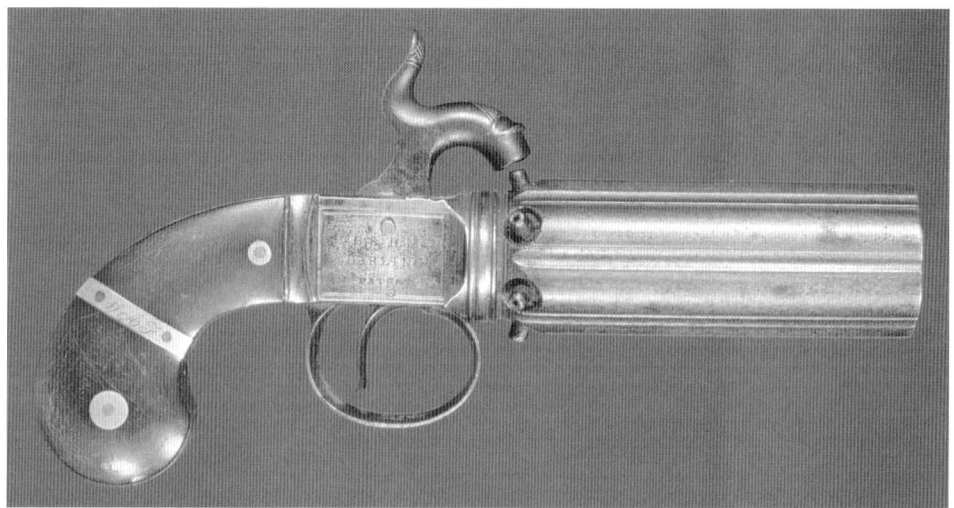

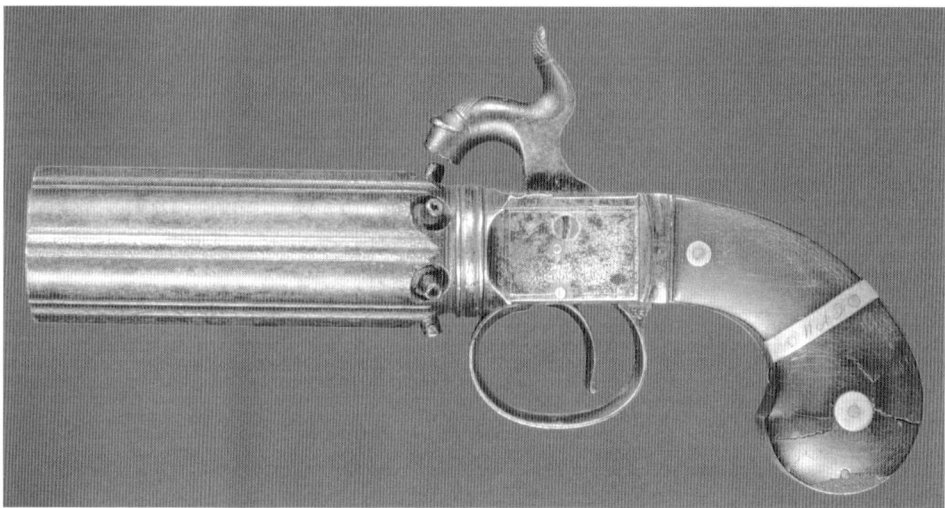

Two overall views of the Darling pepperbox serial number 211. This pistol shows all of the classic Darling features and represents the standard configuration for these pistols. This is an exceedingly attractive pepperbox in original condition with the mechanism still working perfectly.
(Howard Miller collection)

written by that particular company during its years of business. This would leave a gap in the numbers for which there were never any pistols or guns. If we find additional pistols in the low 200s, I will find this "gap" theory much more attractive.

Adding to the quagmire, as discussed earlier, is the fact that some surviving Darlings do not have serial numbers on them. Does this mean that they are early "pre-production" or late "post-production" pieces? Or that they were assigned serial numbers that were never marked on them? Who knows. For the time being, though, I am content with the assumption that there were about one hundred and fifteen or slightly more Darling pepperboxes made. I believe that all the guns in the serial number sequence were pepperbox pistols, and consider number 211 (or however we decide to read those digits) and the unnumbered pistols to be anomalies that do not change the overall count significantly. Perhaps future discoveries will show this to be incorrect, but I think that it is a good working assumption until proven otherwise.

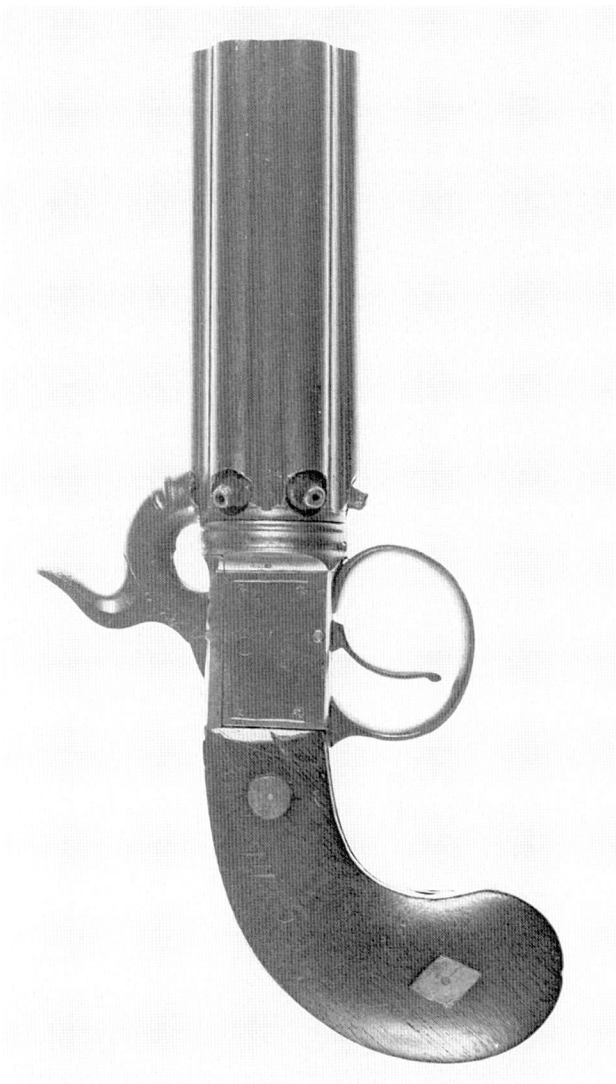

This is an old photograph of a Darling pepperbox once in the William Locke collection. Based on the small dent at the top of the grip, as well as the pistol's overall appearance, I believe that this is the same gun as the previously illustrated Darling with a circled "D" marking. However, since I am not entirely sure, this photograph is being included so that the reader can make his own decision. (Photo courtesy of Robert B. Berryman)

The Darling-Colt Connection

One of the attractions of the Darling for historians and collectors has always been its status as an early rival to the Colt revolver. As described in their patent, Darlings revolve their cylinder (barrel cluster) upon cocking. This is the single most important part of Sam Colt's famous revolver invention and it has been suggested by many that the Darlings were the first to make this revolutionary innovation, despite the fact that Colt received his patent almost two months earlier.

According to Bellingham, Massachusetts' official town history, local fathers have always passed down to their sons the Darling-Colt story. The core of this story or legend is that Benjamin M. Darling went to see his friend Sam Colt in Boston, seeking funds with which to patent and market his newly invented pepperbox pistol. Colt refused to become involved, but when Darling went to patent his invention he found that Colt had just patented the exact same thing, thereby depriving Darling of his fortune. This story has all of the elements of a classic rural myth: a good-hearted local boy is cheated out of his rightful fortune by a duplicitous city slicker with fancy lawyers.

Samuel Colt

While I don't think that the myth described above is exactly true, like most myths it has some basis in fact. We do know that Benjamin M. Darling lived a

Samuel Colt's mansion "Armsmear." Having lived his entire life in small farm houses, rented rooms and finally the asylum for the poor, Benjamin M. Darling must have spent quite a bit of time thinking about "what might have been" if just a few things had gone differently.

long life in the Bellingham/Woonsocket neighborhood, some of which was spent in humiliating poverty. He must have resented Colt's success and doubtless bored all of his acquaintances to death with stories about his "near miss" with fame and riches.

Buying into this, some gun researchers have agreed with the local legend, suggesting that Colt saw a Darling and then used the idea to have his own patent drawn up, with Colt's papers getting submitted more quickly through sloppiness on the Darlings' part and political connections on Colt's. (Note that later reforms in the patent process made patenting of such similar inventions less likely.) The Darling patent was issued on April 13, 1836, and the Colt patent on February 25 of the same year. Some sources even suggest that it was the Darlings, not Colt, who sparked the revolution in gun design seen in the mid-19th century.

While it is fun to think otherwise, it is my belief that this often repeated "chestnut" is an exaggeration. Yes, it is apparent that the Darlings were actually producing pistols before the issue of their patent, but Colt had early working models, too. For those not familiar with the Colt story, he supposedly came up with his ideas on an ocean voyage in 1830–31. By 1832, he was having models and prototypes made, and had filed a caveat for his invention with the U.S. Patent Office, intending to get an actual patent in England first. Colt had the active support of Henry Ellsworth, Commissioner of the U.S. Patent Office.

The first Colt revolver that showed promise was a rifle made in 1832. Further samples and prototypes continued to be made, primarily by gunsmith John Pearson, with the invention developing and maturing

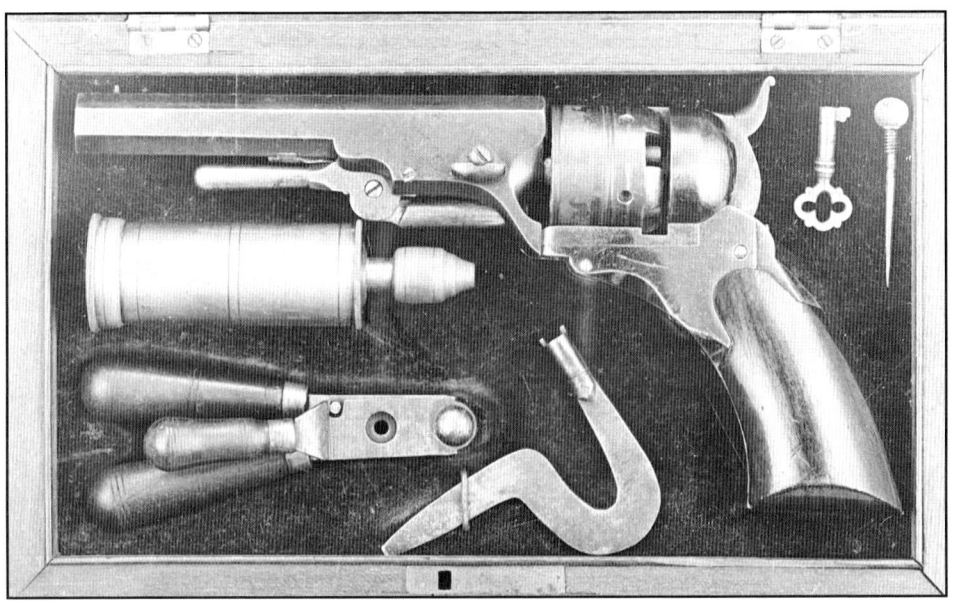

An early Colt revolver made in Paterson, New Jersey. These are the guns that were being designed by Colt at the same time that the Darling brothers were perfecting their own revolver mechanism. While the Darlings initially had a better product, and it may seem like they nearly beat Colt to the punch, the Darling mechanism is only truly useful for pepperboxes, while Colt's design had broader applications and would eventually be effective for anything from pocket pistols to rifles. The Colt design took the world by storm for a reason, and despite Colt's failure at the New Jersey factory, his later success in Hartford seems well deserved in hindsight. (Robert Berryman photo)

over the years. The first "production" guns were made in 1836, the same year that his patent was granted.[52]

While we do not know when the Darlings made their first prototypes, we are certain that the pepperbox was a finished, marketable product when it was patented and probably had required a long period of trial and error, just like the Colt. The time lines for the invention and perfection of the two gun designs were probably quite similar and it is accurate to think of them as rivals because they were working on the same idea at the same time, with great rewards going to the winner. However, as should be clear from the above outline, Colt had developed the basic concept for his invention at an early date and it seems highly unlikely that his original inspiration came from seeing a Darling. This is reinforced by the fact that the Darling's mechanism is vastly different from a Colt; one questions exactly what Colt supposedly copied other than the general concept of the cylinder rotating as part of the cocking process. What seems clear, though, is that the Darlings brought their revolving pistol to market first, and certainly had a more perfected gun at an earlier date. Colt's advantages in legal representation and political connections were real, and it seems quite likely that the Darlings started the patent process first, yet finished last.

Aside from "who came first," it needs to be stressed here that the Colt revolver was a much more promising idea than the Darling pepperbox — despite the many mechanical weaknesses seen in early Colts. Also, Colt himself was a well-connected entrepreneur from a prominent family with powerful and talented friends in the manufacturing and business worlds. The Darlings had none of these advantages. Even if the Darlings had received their patent earlier than Colt, it seems impossible that they ever could have built a gunmaking empire in Woonsocket the way that Colt eventually did in Hartford.

Two published sources have claimed that there was legal action between the Darlings and Colt, and also with Ethan Allen. Much to my surprise, I have found nothing to support this. Noted Colt authority R.L. Wilson has seen no evidence of this kind either, and points out that Colt's lawyers were so good that they were able to intimidate many would-be competitors. He also notes that there are no Darling pepperboxes in Colt's own collections in the Wadsworth Atheneum and the Raymond Baldwin Museum of Connecticut History, even though both collections have other pepperbox pistols. If Colt felt that the Darlings were a challenge, it is likely that he would have owned an example for his own study or for use as a legal exhibit.[53]

Could the Darlings and Colt have met in Boston or elsewhere, as suggested by the local legend? This is entirely possible and perhaps even likely, although there is no known record of it. Colt travelled widely and was an active promoter of his new revolving pistol. Perhaps he even attended the Charitable Mechanic Association Exhibition and Fair in Boston where the Darlings successfully exhibited their pepperbox in 1837. This would certainly explain the Boston meeting passed down as part of the local legend.

Colt was not shy about his invention and loved to talk to clever mechanics about it. Despite their differing backgrounds, the Darlings and Colt would have had much to discuss and, who knows, perhaps they even toyed with the idea of a partnership. But the inventions are so physically different, and Colt's business plan so much more ambitious, that it is easy to see why an agreement would not have been reached.

The Tools in the Darling Probate List

The probate record of Barton Darling discussed earlier (see "The People" section) is the single most important document discovered in the preparation of this book. Lists of tools for working gunmakers are incredibly rare for any era, and the Darling probate inventory is a unique testimony to the gunmaking trade in New England on the cusp of the Industrial Revolution.

      What makes this inventory even more exciting is that it shows that the Darlings had the specific tools required to make each and every part of their pepperbox pistols: lock, stock and barrel, as they say. It was more common for rural New England gunsmiths to bring in specialized parts from outside sources rather than making everything themselves. It was simply inefficient to try to make everything in one shop. However, the Darlings, with a new product that only had a couple of parts that were common to the trade, seem to have made the whole pistol on their own, or at least nearly so.

      Because of the importance of this list, and because many of the objects in it are unknown to the modern reader, an itemized explanation will be attempted below. The author is not an expert on tools and mechanical objects. In fact, he is currently trying to do a simple repair on an antique clock and his chances of success wouldn't be much different if he were trying to launch himself to the moon in a garbage can. Joe Puleo and Peter Schmidt are to be thanked for proofreading this section and for exposing some mistakes that would have been very embarrassing.

Files
Files were the workhorses of the metalworking trade during the 19th century. Any competent metalsmith or mechanic would have had a variety of them in his shop. All of the file types known today were available, including mill files, bastard files, rat tail files and three square files.

Brace & Bits

A brace was a type of hand drill that looked roughly like the capital letter "C" with a handle on top of it for the palm of the hand. Much like the drills of today, it took a variety of bits for different jobs and diameter of the required hole. The Darlings would have used these drills for cutting pin and circular inlay holes in the grips of their pistols. These drills would not have been used to cut through metal. The bits predated the invention of the spiral drill bit (with channels twisting up its length to expel removed material). These earlier bits, called "flat" drill bits, had two cutting surfaces on their tip and plain sides. They cut very efficiently and were easy to sharpen, but had difficulty cutting deep holes because they would quickly jam. Every few moments, the drill bit would have to be removed from the hole, which would have to be cleared (usually by blowing into it).

Files

More files as already listed and described.

Jamb Plate & Taps

Taps were used for cutting female (internal) screw threads in holes that needed to receive machine screws. The Darlings used a great deal of maleable iron and low carbon steel, which are very friendly raw materials for tap work, and there were holes in their pistols that needed to be threaded for the insertion of screws. Prior to 1870, most taps were made with a tapered diameter and resembled the body of a screw or bolt, with a sharp spiral land and groove and segmented flutes running lengthwise to allow for the chips cut from the metal plate to be pushed out of the way. Taps were made with a specified number of turns, which are known today as threads per inch or t.p.i. Once the tap was backed out after cutting the thread, a screw or bolt could then be inserted if it had the proper threads per inch. The reason that taps were tapered in historical times was so that they could be used to cut many different diameters of holes with just one tool. Today each tap in a set of taps is made to a specific diameter and many more taps are required in order to make up a full set.

    A Jamb Plate was probably a simple device for making threaded machine screws. Mechanics in those days would take a soft piece of steel and tap a threaded hole in it. Then they would harden the piece of steel. Screws blanks could now be threaded by forcing them into the threaded hole...in effect, jamming them (or in antiquated spelling "jambing" them) into the mold. This ensured regularity in the screws because all the threading would be identical to the mold and each screw would be sure to fit other threaded holes made with the same tap.

Sundries
Various things of little value.

Screws & Nails
Obvious.

1 Box & Contents
Obvious.

Copper Kettle & contents
Obvious.

1 pr Tinmans Shears
Heavy, scissor-like tools for cutting sheet metal. They are often used today for duct work in forced air heating and air conditioning systems. The Darlings probably used these for cutting the attractive german silver inlays seen on their grips.

Types
A metal die set including the alphabet and numbers, which would have been used for stamping words and serial numbers on the frames of the pepperbox pistols.

Shot & Lead
Bullets and the raw material for making them.

Lot of old trumpery
Trumpery is showy but worthless finery, and can also mean rubbish. In this context, it probably means scrap iron with no immediate potential for use.

1 Smith's Anvil
Obvious.

one vice
Obvious.

1 Turning engine
The gearworks that harnessed the spinning power of the turbine so that it could be used by the lathe and other machinery.

1 Turning Lathe
Like today, a lathe was a work horse of a machine tool that spun metal or wood on a horizontal axis so that it could be cut and shaped. The material being worked, not the tool, moved, which gave this piece of machinery a great deal of power and precision. The Darlings would have used a lathe to reduce steel bars into round barrels for their cylinders or barrel clusters.

12 prs. hand screws
Perhaps screw drivers, but why would they come in pairs? Maybe because each brother had his own set? Another explanation would be that they were small clamps used to hold components during filing, drilling or shaping work.

2 Smith's vices
A blacksmith's vice is one that can be operated by the smith's leg when his hands are otherwise occupied. Sometimes called a leg vice.

Blacksmith's Tools
Too vague for explanation. Probably hammers, tongs, etc.

Arbours & Reams
An arbour, sometimes called a mandrel, is the live spindle of a turning lathe. Fitted into a hole reamed smooth they would allow the outside dimensions to be machined in perfect alingment with the inside ones. Reams are instruments with cutting or scraping edges, used with a twisting motion, for enlarging and smoothing a round hole in metal or wood. Reams would have been used in lathe work, accurately smoothing the inside of drilled holes.

Anvil & Iron
The iron listed here seems to be bar iron from which the pistol parts

were shaped.

Files, Lathe Buff Wheel & Lathing Engine
These appear to be the tools that the Darlings used for finishing and polishing metal after rough fabrication was finished. The lathing engine was probably smaller than the turning engine listed above and would have spun the buffing wheel.

Grindstone
Something to keep your nose to. The Darlings would have used this for grinding metal parts into their roughly finished shapes and for sharpening tools.

Upright drilling Lathe
Equivalent of the modern drill press. This would have been used to cut the barrels and axle into the solid cylinders.

Fluting Engine
The machine used to cut the exterior shape into the solid cylinders. The flutes on Darling pepperbox cylinders are attractive and consistent. This quality of work could only have been accomplished using a machine that allowed "indexing" (consistently and accurately turning) the cylinder on its long axis. This machine probably included the features of another common 19th-century metalworking tool, the "shaper," which was an extremely sturdy planing tool that allowed irregular curved profiles to be cut with great accuracy.

one work bench
Where you sit while you work.

1 Ash Plank, 80ft.
Anyone able to explain this one has my admiration. Eighty feet is a very long plank, so perhaps it is actually square feet, which would make more sense. Ash is an exceptionally hard wood that was common in New England during the 19th century.

Bibliography

Published Sources

Achtermier, William O., *Rhode Island Arms Makers and Gunsmiths, 1643–1883*. Mowbray Publishing, Lincoln, RI, 1980.

Arnold, James N., *Vital Record of Rhode Island, 1636-1850*. Published Under the Auspices of the General Assembly, Providence, 1892.

Ashede, Eric, "Smaländske Mässingsvapen," *Samlarnytt*, No. 7/8, 1963.

Bayles, Richard M., ed., *History of Providence County, Rhode Island*. W.W. Preston & Co., New York, 1891.

Bazelon, Bruce S., and McGuinn, William F., *Directory of American Military Goods Dealers and Makers*, combined 1999 edition. Self-published and available from *Man at Arms* magazine.

Blair, Claude, ed., *Pollard's History of Firearms*. Macmillan Publishing Co., New York, 1983.

Daniels, A.S., *Statistics of the Village of Woonsocket, 1842*. Printed in Woonsocket by Mason & Vose.

Dunlap, Jack, *American British and Continental Pepperbox Firearms*. Privately published, 1964, later reprinted by Pacific Books, 1967.

Dunlap, H.J., "The So-Called Brass Frame Darling Pepperbox," *The Gun Report*, June 1966.

Glockner, Marty, "The Darling Brothers Rotary Pistol," The *Crimpville Comments* #101, Bellingham Historical Commission, 1976.

Horner, Frank R., "Pepperboxes," A.S.A.C. *Bulletin*, #11, 1965.

Howard, Robert, *Water Power: How it Works*. Eleutherian Mills — Hagley Foundation, Inc., 1979.

Jillson, David, *Genealogy of the Gillson and Jillson Family*. E.L. Freeman & Co., Central Falls, RI, 1876.

Miller, Howard, Jr., "Two darling Darlings," PAGCA *Monthly Bugle*, November 1998.

Mouillesseaux, Harold R., *Ethan Allen, Gunmaker: His Partners, Patents & Firearms*. Museum Restoration Service, Ottawa, Canada 1973.

Newman, Sylvanus C., *A Numbering of the Inhabitants of Woonsocket, 1846*. Printed by S.S. Foss.

Palmer, Andy, "First U.S. Pepperbox Pistol Was Made In Bellingham,"

The *Crimpville Comments*, June 1974.
Partridge, George F., *History of the Town of Bellingham, Massachusetts 1719–1919*. Town of Bellingham, 1919.
Richardson, Erastus, *History of Woonsocket*, 1905.
Smith, Sam E., "The Darling Pepperbox," *The Gun Report*, January 1942.
Smith, Sam E., "South Carolina Ante-Bellum Pistols," *The American Rifleman*, and later reprinted in *The Gun Report*, November 1955.
Smith, Sam E., "Probing the Questionable," The A.S.A.C. *Bulletin*, #13.
Taft, Ernie, *The Town of Bellingham Massachusetts*. Privately printed 1997.
Thomas, Dr. Alton P., *Woonsocket: Highlights of History, 1800–1976*. Published by the Woonsocket Opera House Society, 1976.
Winant, Lewis, *Pepperbox Firearms*. Greenberg Publisher, New York, 1952.

Unpublished, Government and Archival Sources

Bellingham Massachusetts Town Records, at the Bellingham Town Hall Clerk's Office.
Edgar J. Allaire Papers in the Woonsocket Harris Public Library.
Handwritten census ledgers in the collections of the Rhode Island Historical Society.
"History of Woonsocket," an unpublished manuscript in the Woonsocket Public Library.
First Exhibition and Fair of the Massachusetts Charitable Mechanic Association, at Faneuil and Quincy Halls, in the City of Boston, September 18, 1837. (A listing of the exhibits and prizes.)
The Journal of the Franklin Institute.
The Norfolk County, Massachusetts, Land Record Books.
The Pawtucket and Woonsocket Directory, 1857, William H. Boyd Publisher, New York.
The Pawtucket, Central Falls and Woonsocket Directory, Webb Bros., Providence, 1869.
Smithfield, Rhode Island, Land Evidence Books for Grantor and Grantee, now located in the vault at the Central Falls City Clerk's office.
Town of Bellingham, Massachusetts, Land Record Books.
The Bellingham, Massachusetts, Military Census of May 1, 1840, in the Bellingham Town Records.

The Darling Pepperbox

Town of Cumberland, Rhode Island, Land Evidence Books.
Town of Cumberland, Rhode Island, Probate Books.
Vital Records of Bellingham, Mass., to the Year 1850. New England
    Historic Genealogical Society, Boston, MA, 1904.
Woonsocket Black List for 1882.
The *Woonsocket Patriot* newspaper.
Woonsocket, Rhode Island, Tax books and Directories.
1777 Military Census of Cumberland Rhode Island

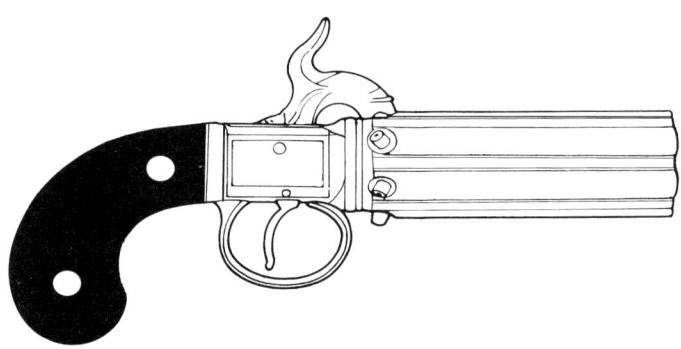

Endnotes

1. The Providence Almanac quoted in "History of Woonsocket," an unpublished manuscript in the Woonsocket Public Library.
2. Quoted from *Woonsocket: Highlights of History, 1800–1976* by Dr. Alton P. Thomas and published by the Woonsocket Opera House Society, 1976.
3. Arnold, James N., *Vital Record of Rhode Island, 1636–1850*, Published Under the Auspices of the General Assembly, Providence, 1892. This source lists the bride's name as Levinia (notice the different spelling), daughter of Nathan, and records that the marriage was performed by Jotham Carpenter, justice. From these same vital records, it appears that the groom was born on July 23, 1774, in Cumberland, but Benjamin was a common name in the family and I have been unable to confirm this birth date.
4. Jillson, David. *Genealogy of the Gillson and Jillson Family*. E.L. Freeman & Co., Central Falls, RI, 1876, p. 44. The Darling family lived in Cumberland at least back to the time of the Revolution, at which point I stopped looking. Benjamin's father and grandfather (Benjamin M. and Barton's grandfather and great-grandfather), who were both named Peter, are listed in the *1777 Military Census of Cumberland Rhode Island* (p. 29). The younger Peter is listed as between 16 and 50 years of age and able-bodied; the elder Peter is listed as over 60 and therefore not eligible for service. Benjamin is listed as a "mechanic."
5. According to Jillson, the full list of children (in order of birth) was: Barton (b. July 31, 1799; d. July 6, 1848), Newton (b. Feb. 14, 1802; d. Aug. 4, 1803), Alvin (b. May 16, 1804; d. May 11, 1856), Susan (b. Jan. 6, 1807), Benjamin M. (b. Sept. 29, 1809), Eliza (b. Oct. 8, 1812; d. Dec. 23, 1818) and William P. (b. Aug. 7, 1816; d. June 21, 1818). Note that Newton, Eliza and William died as children.
6. Handwritten census ledgers in the collections of the Rhode Island Historical Society.
7. Town of Cumberland Land Evidence Book #9, page 218, shows Benjamin purchasing two tracts of land from Nathan Arnold.
8. Town of Cumberland Land Evidence Book #9, page 365. The purchase was from Bani Bartlett, and since the parcel was landlocked from the road, Darling was assigned the rights to pass to his shop through the land of his neighbor Esuk Cook, who also appears to have operated a shop at that location.
9. Town of Cumberland Probate Book #18, p. 175, lists an inventory of his estate.
10. Various Rhode Island and Massachusetts Land Evidence Books.
11. Town of Cumberland Land Evidence Book #6, page 12, and #10, page 500. Also see Norfolk County, MA Land Record Book #64, folio 76.
12. Bellingham Town Records, Vol. 4, p. 129, found at the Bellingham Town Hall Clerk's Office and listed as part of the highway inspection and repair budget for 1835.
13. Norfolk County Land Record Book #110, folio 15.
14. Norfolk County Land Record Book #116, folio 101 and Book 112, folio 300 for example.
15. *Vital Records of Bellingham, Mass., to the Year 1850*. New England Historic Genealogical Society, Boston, MA, 1904. Also noted in the "Darling Family Genealogy," an unpublished manuscript by Paul A. Darling in the Bellingham Public Library historical archives. This was not the first engagement published for Barton Darling; on March 21, 1830, he had published his intention to marry Martha W. Paine, but the outcome of this relationship is unknown.
16. Alvin was born May 16, 1804 and died May 11, 1856.
17. *Journal of the Franklin Institute*, November 1835, p. 311, "American Patents for April with Remarks." From the collection of the Hagley Library courtesy Robert Howard.
18. *Woonsocket Patriot*, first week of January 1837, "A Census of Woonsocket, Taken in

December 1836." This listing of the city's inhabitants numbers the Alvin Darling household as having two males over 10, two females over 10, and 4 children under 10.

[19] Smithfield Land Evidence Books for Grantor and Grantee, now located in the vault at the Central Falls City Clerk's office. The initial lease is dated October 20, 1836 and had a term of ten years with options for renewals. The owner of the land, Spencer Mowry, was to be paid fifteen dollars yearly, starting on the first day of April 1837. This lease begins at exactly the same time that the water wheel advertisements stop, probably indicating that he had rented before but was now securing a leasehold for a future venture unrelated to waterwheel production. The land is described as bordering land of the Globe Manufacturing Company, John J. Paine and Alden Coe, "bound together with the water power to the same belonging." Alvin had to promise not to sell "ardent spirits" on the property and there were lengthy provisions for how Alvin would be reimbursed for his buildings and improvements should the lease not be renewed. Other transactions regarding this lease are found in Book 22, #77, and Book 25, #286. This last entry is for the exact same land but lists Willing Vose as a further neighbor. In an unrelated note that doesn't seem to fit anywhere else, one of Alvin's children, a George Darling, died in the Globe neighborhood on January 21, 1869, at the age of 35.

[20] While the numbers from these early patents were removed in future years because of confusion resulting from the patent office fire, arms researcher Frank Sellers has determined that the original number of this patent was #9,591X by checking against documents at the Franklin Institute.

[21] First Exhibition and Fair of the Massachusetts Charitable Mechanic Association, at Faneuil and Quincy Halls, in the City of Boston, September 18, 1837. Dutton and Wentworth, Boston, 1837, p. 31. This booklet was made available to me through the kindness of arms researcher Nick Chandler.

[22] While William Glaze is perhaps best known for his operations closer to the time of the Civil War, he was indeed active when Darling pepperboxes were being made. From 1838 until 1841, for instance, he was in partnership with John Veal. See Bruce Bazelon's *American Military Goods Dealers and Makers*.

[23] Town of Bellingham Land Record Book #124, folio 33.

[24] The Bellingham Military Census of May 1, 1840, in the Bellingham Town Records does not list them and certainly would have had they still been living there.

[25] Town of Cumberland Land Evidence Book #17, page 85. I have been unable to locate this exact property since Waldo Earle owned many lots of land in Woonsocket and the description is vague. However, the "highway heading from the village to Mendon" is the present-day North Main Street.

[26] Town of Cumberland Land Evidence Book #17, page 197.

[27] Barton Darling's household is listed in *Statistics of the Village of Woonsocket, 1842*, by A.S. Daniels, printed in Woonsocket by Mason & Vose. He is also listed in Sylvanus C. Newman's *A Numbering of the Inhabitants of Woonsocket, 1846*, printed by S.S. Foss. This 1846 listing shows him in Woonsocket proper (rather than in one of the many outlying neighborhoods). His age is listed as forty-six, and his household was composed of four adults, two male and two female, which may indicate that Benjamin M. was boarding with him. His other brother Alvan Darling is listed as forty-two years of age and living in the Globe neighborhood, doubtless on the leased land across the river in Smithfield mentioned earlier.

[28] Erastus Richardson, *A History of Woonsocket*, 1905.

[29] *History of Providence County, Rhode Island*, edited by Richard M. Bayles, W.W. Preston & Co., New York, 1891, pp. 271–272. The cannon are deserving of additional mention, since they had been captured during the Revolution from Gen. Burgoyne, and later given to the United Train of Artillery (from whom the Dorrites later stole them) by Gen. Washington.

[30] Town of Cumberland Land Evidence Book #20, page 266. The burial plot, marked 30A, was located in the village of Woonsocket and purchased from Joseph Smith. This plot has not been identified, but may have been in Oak Hill Cemetery, which was the popular graveyard in Woonsocket during the 19th century. Many of the Darlings and their relations

31. Town of Cumberland Probate Book #18, page 239 and 248.
32. Town of Cumberland Probate Book #18, page 233.
33. Bazelon, p. 256.
34. Alvin Darling's lease with Spencer Mowry was discussed in an earlier note and included extensive provisions for what would happen, should the lease not be extended, to buildings and improvements Alvin intended to make to the land. In short, an appraisal would be done on these structures and Alvin would be compensated in cash. On August 25, 1842, Alvin ended the lease and was paid $94 for the "buildings standing." He was allowed the right to renew the lease at its original terms any time within two years if he was able to pay back the $94. This seems to have been accomplished, because on June 6, 1848 the lease (for the exact same land description) was terminated by Alvin again, this time with compensation of $100. This is the transaction that took place right before Barton's death and not only included the "buildings standing" but "water power and water wheel and all the gearing there unto belonging."
35. Smithfield Land Evidence Book 20, #249.
36. *The Pawtucket and Woonsocket Directory, 1857*, William H. Boyd Publisher, New York; and the *History of Providence County*, pp. 287-188, and the *History of Providence County*, pp. 287–288.
37. *The Pawtucket, Central Falls and Woonsocket Directory*, Webb Bros., Providence, 1869. See the 1869–70, 1871 and 1872 editions. He is not listed in the 1873 edition.
38. Darling Pond is still there, but all the houses in this area were removed some time ago to make way for a Wal-Mart and a series of shopping centers. Darling Pond is a very small body of water, barely noticeable next to an Applebees restaurant.
39. Woonsocket Tax books and Directories for 1882–1896. The gunsmiths included Edwin A. Darling and the two brothers Edmund R. and Barton L. Darling. Barton L. Darling (who was previously listed as a boarder) appears to have inherited or been given the property c.1882, living there with his wife Alice until 1895, when they moved to a house at 4 Spring Street. According to his obituary, he was soon removed to the State Insane Asylum in Cranston where he died on April 8, 1895. His widow continued to live at the Spring Street address and his wake was held there. Edmund R. Darling, who was born on April 10, 1853, operated a gunsmith/locksmith/hardware/sporting goods store on Main Street in Woonsocket from about 1873 until his death in 1921. For more details about this younger generation of Darling gunsmiths, refer to the Edgar J. Allaire Papers in the Woonsocket Harris Public Library. As will be noted, gunsmithing and locksmithing are related trades and many men practiced both in order to make a living. It might interest the reader that until 2002 there was a Darling Cycle and Lock Shop in Woonsocket on 215 Arnold St., indicating that the family tradition continued into the 21st century. Unfortunately, not a single one of the many living members of the Darling family responded to advertisements and surveys sent out by the author seeking information about earlier generations of their family.
40. Despite Benjamin M. Darling's poverty, it is interesting that he is not listed in the incredibly lengthy *Woonsocket Black List* for 1882, which is an actual typeset book printed by local merchants that lists people considered a credit risk.
41. Each year, Woonsocket's Overseer of Poor, John H. Lee, made a detailed report of all relief provided to city residents. This might be cash, firewood, food, a train ticket to attend a distant family event or burial expenses. Sometimes payments were in cash, other times the payments were made directly to a merchant. These are the items listed for Benjamin M. Darling for each fiscal year ending April 30: 1882/to Bailey E. Boyden for rent, 16.00; to C.W. Paine for milk, 4.00. 1883/to E.M. Stockwell for supplies, 39.20; cash, 25.00. 1884/to E.M. Stockwell for supplies, 13.68; to Richard Barnett for supplies, 104.00; cash, 10.00. 1887/ cash, 1.50; cash, 87.00; to Jerome Kennedy, 3.00. 1888/cash, 119.00.
42. Coe Street numbers known to have been owned by Darlings are 262 and 322.
43. Respected local historian Ernie Taft has told me in conversation that "real old-timers" used

to say that the pistol factory had been "right below the rake factory near the brook." Even if this is correct, the distance between the rake factory site and the brook is mere feet, so the distinction is minor. Also, the maps do not show a mill site right on the brook, with both possible sites being up from the brook on land that would not have flooded in spring, which better matches the rake factory site as described.

44 Sam Smith, who kept careful records of all the interesting guns he saw or heard about, would eventually become aware of at least three total examples of the true Darling, one owned by Carl Metzger, one sold by the dealer Serven to a collector in California, and another in a Rhode Island collection (personal letter from Smith to Louis Winant, September 18, 1950.) Within a few more years his list of reported "first model" Darlings would grow to seven.

45 Smith, Sam E., "Probing the Questionable," A.S.A.C. Bulletin #13.

46 At a time when nice Allen pepperboxes were selling for $6, these "brass Darlings" were getting $50.

47 For further discussion of these Swedish pistols, see Eric Ashede's article "Smaländske Mässingsvapen," in Samlarnytt, No. 7/8, 1963.

48 The initials AGS found on many of the brass pistols stands for Anders Gustafsson, who worked for Engholm and later married his employer's daughter Johanna in 1869. The initials AIS stand for Anders Johannesson who also originally worked for Engholm but later went into a similar business for himself. The initials IEH are thought to indicate Engholm himself.

49 Not to be confused with the rag wheels used for buffing and polishing today, in the 19th century, rag wheels were large gears used in saw mills to pull the logs through the saw.

50 Numerous theories have been circulated concerning this Glaze pistol, none of them entirely satisfactory. Many collectors feel that it was made by Glaze as a copy of the Darling design, perhaps under license from the inventors. This is unlikely, because Glaze was generally just a seller and not a maker of the various items that bear his name. At least one very knowledgeable antique gun dealer has suggested that the Glaze pistol is probably a fake perpetrated upon Sam Smith by his collecting rival William Locke. This is a colorful and intriguing theory, which would go a long way towards explaining the extended cylinder, the unusual grips and the irregular hammer. However, I have examined this pistol personally and because of the kindness of its current owner was allowed to take it entirely apart. If it is a fake, then it is a very convincing one. The lock and mechanism, in particular, appear to be genuine. I can say nothing regarding the originality of the "Glaze" markings because I did not have high magnification available, but I could see no reason to doubt them. The fit, finish and inner workings are all as would be expected on a genuine Darling with the exception of the parts already noted. Given its condition, perhaps a useful explanation of this gun is that it may have been heavily restored, including replaced grips and hammer.

51 The subject of whether advertising stopped permanently is a tricky one. While the advertisements were indeed discontinued in 1839, there are a chunk of years missing from the records of the Woonsocket Patriot newspaper during the 1840s, and it is impossible to say for sure that advertising was never resumed.

52 While the above details can be found in many books about firearms and Colts, readers wanting to read more are specifically directed to those written by R.L. Wilson.

53 Letter to the author from R.L. Wilson, dated November 14, 1997.